The AI Memory Machine

The AI Memory Machine

Why the past is all over

ANDREW HOSKINS
KRISTÍNA ČIMOVÁ
AND
DANNY PILKINGTON

OXFORD
UNIVERSITY PRESS

OXFORD
UNIVERSITY PRESS

Great Clarendon Street, Oxford, OX2 6DP,
United Kingdom

Oxford University Press is a department of the University of Oxford.
It furthers the University's objective of excellence in research, scholarship,
and education by publishing worldwide. Oxford is a registered trade mark of
Oxford University Press in the UK and in certain other countries.

Published in the United States of America by Oxford University Press
546 Fifth Avenue, New York, NY 10036, United States of America

British Library Cataloguing in Publication Data
Data available

Library of Congress Control Number: 2026938320

ISBN 9780198995906

DOI: 10.1093/oso/9780198995906.001.0001

The manufacturer's authorized representative in the EU for product safety is
Oxford University Press España S.A. of Parque Empresarial San Fernando de Henares,
Avenida de Castilla, 2 – 28830 Madrid (www.oup.es/en or product.safety@oup.com).
OUP España S.A. also acts as importer into Spain of products made by the manufacturer.

Contents

Acknowledgements

We are indebted to all the expert memory app and service designers, CEOs, and journalists, who generously gave up their time and who informed our research in many ways, including: Jacob Appel, Ryan Calo, Lauren Goode, Cesar Kuriyama, Matt Raoul, Jonathan Wegener, and Laura Guien.

We are very grateful to the constructive and detailed help and advice on this work from three anonymous reviewers on this work and to Martin Baum and colleagues at Oxford University Press for their great support. The founding work for this project was enabled by a University of Glasgow COVID research grant awarded in 2021 to Andrew and Kristína.

There are many friends and colleagues who are a constant source of inspiration and support in our research and writing, and we are particularly indebted to: Catherine Happer, William Merrin, Amanda Barnier, Ben O'Loughlin, Anthony Downey, Luli van der Does, Kate Wright, and Emma Flynn.

1
The Machine Gets Personal

Introduction

Nothing is left alone anymore! All of life is augmented; no encounter or experience is left unrecorded or unshared. Silence and contemplation are the enemies of the digitisation and datafication of everything; whole societies are being scooped up to train transformer models. Everyone has become a hybridised cipher of the present and their pasts, sifting, tagging, sharing, and riding the flux of messages, images, and videos, reproducing themselves.

Is this the final, and fatal collapse, of past into present? After Big Data's swamping of the self, politics, culture, and economy, will AI slop finish the job and bury all that is human about memory?

What kind of reality will be findable, usable again, as any kind of meaningful past? Will your memory of tomorrow be determined by what you snap, click, swipe, send, and feed today? Is your future already anticipated and predicted from a past that you have already produced and shared, knowingly and unknowingly, over the course of your smartphone life? What will become of the digitally produced, app-scattered, AI-assembled you? What kind of memory is this?

Today's defining technologies of memory—digital apps, platforms, services—turbocharged by generative AI (GAI), operate at new complexity and scale, sensing, capturing, and mining the *individual* as the pre-eminent commodity of this age. Here we arrive at the essence of the AI memory *machine*, in that something traditionally defined through not being human has triumphed precisely through its personalisation, its convincing anthropomorphism, and its grasp of you.

The AI memory machine is the capitalist-induced revolution in the individual, social, and the technological forging of memory. This is not

The AI Memory Machine. Andrew Hoskins, Kristína Čimová, and Danny Pilkington,
Oxford University Press.
DOI: 10.1093/oso/9780198995906.003.0001

only a matter of how shifts in the external world enhance or diminish human memory. Rather, it is how an entire emergent digital media ecology shapes software, platforms, and algorithm owners and designers' imaginaries as to what remembering actually is in the twenty-first century and how it can remain a profitable commodity.

It is useful to see the arrival of the machinic grasp of you as a new and different phase of that which Mumford (1934) historicised as the relationship between 'technics and civilisation'. Instead of attributing ultimate power to externalised forces of a kind of separate or independent system, Mumford finds the machine as a 'product of human ingenuity and effort' and existing 'as an element of human culture' (1934, 6). But has Mumford's championing of human choice as the dominant feature of what later theorists saw as an 'ecology'[1] or environment of media been subverted in the digital era?

Certainly, human dependency on and addiction to the smartphone and social media would seem to suggest so. Digital devices, platforms, and services have fundamentally reshaped the process through which memories are made and stored. Our memories are mediated by a technological lens that we are dependent on to evidence and make sense of ourselves and the world (Jungselius & Weilenmann 2023, Hoskins & Halstead 2021). And this lens, tinted by the platforms we use, is one of infinite personalisation and apparent choice. For instance, Viljoen, Goldenfein, and McGuigan (2021) characterise this lens as generated by a process of 'mechanism design' supposedly aimed at optimising individuals and society by creating the conditions for complete autonomy and rationality. An apolitical, transcendental, technological solution? Not quite:

> Under the legitimising glow of mechanism design, companies like Google and Facebook have optimised their platforms to accumulate information, capital, and managerial control ... installing automated market-like institutions to orchestrate social choices and allocate opportunities and value across more and more settings (Viljoen, Goldenfein & McGuigan 2021, 2)

This book takes one of these settings as *memory*. In the age of platform capitalism, data is the most valuable and exploitable commodity (Walton

& Nayak 2021), and we are its wellsprings. Dependent on platforms for remembering and being remembered, our memories have become both the fuel and the crystallisation of capitalism's goal to optimise us as customers. Byung-Chul Han (2017, 34–35) for instance, argues,

> The smartphone promises more freedom, but it radiates a fatal compulsion—the compulsion to communicate. Now an almost obsessive, compulsive relationship to digital devices prevails ... Social networks magnify such compulsion to communicate on a massive scale. More communication means more capital. In turn, the accelerated circulation of communication and information leads to the accelerated circulation of capital.

And it is the emergent forms of this capital, which Matz (2025, 62) calls 'behavioural residue', including that accumulated from, for instance, 'Google searches, spending records, and smartphone sensors', that we take to constitute the greatest memorial vulnerability of our age.

The terrible paradox of the memory machine is that it has produced the most awesome archive of human existence ever created while putting this same archive beyond individual human comprehension. Yet this is precisely the requirement for reasserting human control, argued by Mumford, 'In order to reconquer the machine and subdue it to human purposes, one must first understand and assimilate it' (1934, 6). Instead, GAI is the supreme reverser of this relationship between us knowing the machine and the machine knowing us.

For instance, Sam Altman declared on X how ChatGPT's improvements in memory was something to get excited about, and thus 'AI systems ... get to know you over your life, and become extremely useful and personalized' (Altman 2025). Yet this is not some kind of hidden human handing over of personal data, their conversations, or their memory in the making, but is rather a promoted feature of the machine. Share with us everything and we will help you remember it.

The digital generation, Generation F—for Forget—are producing a paradoxical archive of the self. It is nowhere, yet everywhere; given away for free, yet it is one of the most valuable commodities of our time. The 'F' for forget is a paradox. The individual human ability to know, recognise, remember, and to forget has not only been outsourced but also duplicated—you are no longer unique as a remembering agent.

The long tech-promised fiction and fantasy of control over a 'superhuman memory' (Hoskins 2026) is delivered, yes, but at a fatal cost to what made memory human in the first place. The price is exactly the uniqueness that comes with individual experience as something cognitively achieved, willed and deliberative, in the head, but also the mind's supreme protection of someone with the capacity, consciously and unconsciously, to forget.

The past then is *all over* in the mass overproduction, sharing, storing, and mining of information and data about human experience, views, and relationships, that accumulates archives of new complexity and scale. This same abundance pushes memory beyond individual human control in how we are made knowable and memorable, but also how we can remember and forget, is shaped through new tech dependencies and addictions.

Before the AI memory machine

Sometime in the mid-2000s, we no longer had to look or search for things; Google became the portal that took the 'private' out of private detective. Overnight, digital media resurrected the decaying and misplaced past and connected us again with old school friends, former lovers, and all that could and should have been forgotten. The past was suddenly laid bare, in all its digital glory, grime, and gore. In addition to enabling twenty-first century surveillance, this new exposure of the past has been deployed to help distract from and smooth over our present insecurities. As Furedi (2013, 33) argues, 'the project of excavating the past is motivated by an instinct to evade the present'.

Societies have often recast their pasts considering present needs—but today an accumulating digital glut enables them to be used and abused by all-comers. Instead of guiding the present, the past is run through the intoxicating and toxic algorithms of our time, sucked up by distorted polarisation, division, and exclusion, a new radicalisation of memory (Hoskins 2026). It seems inescapable, unerasable, like a new burden the present is made to carry.

This is a highly individualised and personalised burden. Our virtual selves are not only documented and remembered, but they are increasingly obsessed over, their *vibe* considered not only a representation but also *the* representation of their human subject. As such, virtual selves demand new forms of care. But when memory becomes something rendered through digital feeds, connectivity, and networks, is it ever possible to disconnect, delete, and erase any part of your autobiography that is already published, already shared, yourself in the ether?

Memory has always been a process, rather than something that is ever over or complete, an object or a store. Remembering is a conundrum of being always unfinished in its remaking in ever-new moments, new contexts, yet which is familiar and recognisable as something that has been experienced before.

Technologies and media of every era have long aided but also messed with this process, capturing, representing, duplicating, archiving, fixing, monetising, warping, finding, obscuring, and cheating, but also losing, the past. From cave paintings to writing to the earliest photograph to the first flickering moving pictures, to radio, talkies, early BBC television, network national programming, linked transmissions like the early Eurovision song contests, to the relentless information saturation of satellite news organisations, there is a history to the accelerating forces of ways to represent, imagine, store, connect, and replay and revision events and experiences.

The twentieth century is seen as exceptional in its accelerating and connecting the mass technologies and media of memory, via an entwining of the electronic audiovisual technologies of representation, broadcast, and archiving, with a new will to remember. This included through intensifying public and political engagement with the memory of catastrophe, including the premiere screening of the Holocaust television miniseries on NBC in 1978 (Shandler 1999). However, the trend in the spreading of multiple voices of past difficult histories became more competitive and compulsive, with a shift from a sense of responsibility to obligation, accelerated by the news cycles sucking up the commemoration of everything.

This 'broadcast era' (Merrin 2014) was foundational in shaping perceptions, concepts, and ideas on how media shaped memory. It is important to recognise here how media are epistemological engines: they create our experience, knowledge, concepts of truth, and horizons of thought (Merrin & Hoskins 2025). This includes the last century's mass media fostering of a kind of shared experience or reality that many assumed resulted in the forging of 'collective memory' (Hoskins 2025).

These ideas spilled over into the twenty-first century to give the impression of the digital velocity of linking, liking, sharing, as something social, as a somehow unifying experience of a mass action or mass movement, and as the bearing of a new form of collective memory. In short, being awash with media was mistaken for being awash with memory, something presumed to be accessible and to endure, beyond human and group presence.

Whereas the media of the twentieth century produced content for us, the audience, to consume, in this century there has been a fundamental reversal in this relationship, as social media platforms not only shape the swathes of content we consume, but they also give us the tools to produce content of our own to distribute all that is personal and once protected in disconnected and private spheres.

There was a tipping point in our relationship with digital media and technologies around the end of the 2000s and early 2010s, namely the 'connective turn' (Hoskins 2011). This was a shift from individual and societal reliance, to a dependency, on digital mechanisms and services for the making and the losing of memory. A more recent tipping point is the 2020's shift to more addictive relations with AI-generated services and human duplicates (digital twins and deadbots), constituting a new kind of memory in the wild.

The media machinic capture of the human to represent in and to remake as memory in some ways is not new. For instance, the most individually unique of human features, the face, is intimately tied to autobiographical, familial, and generational memory through its photographic capture, reproduction, storage, framing, representation and display, and later human recognition and remembrance, but also its covering up, erasure, and denial. This process of the photographic remaking of memory operated at different scales across the twentieth century, circulating within a given group said to be defining the limits of 'collective memory' (Halbwachs 1980) or an image of celebrity or human catastrophe rendered iconic through its recirculation over generations.

The AI industry of memory

This century is undoubtedly marked by the individual producing and sharing data and information about themselves, but also the self *being* produced and shared. This has wrecked any sense of a boundary between the individual or collective, the private and the public, through effectively ending that condition once known as anonymity, through a new kind of memorial vulnerability. As Basar, Coupland and Obrist (2021, 79) in their exposition of *The Extreme Self*, put it, 'There's a shitload of money to be made in identifying every face that's ever been uploaded'.

The AI memory machine has facilitated our feeding of it, given our experience that compared with a pre-digital era, so little seems to evade capture. The past is all over in that the vast accumulation of a kind of new 'museum of the real' (Merrin 2021) is something that has been waiting to open its doors to welcome in visitors to be amazed by its treasures. These treasures appear as strangely familiar, uncanny, in that this new kind of memory is constituted from our datafied and digital lives and trails.

Perhaps the most efficient means to make sense of this scattered self is already to ask an AI assistant or companion to recall information about ourselves, *for* ourselves. If there is a digital trace, and the machine decides it is relevant, everything will be available for apparent recall. But in a world of fragmented memories, who gets to decide which shards are kept? The risk here is to a humanly willed memory, namely to intentionality:

> It's not a perfectly rosy future, because we still have to trust the companies that ultimately decide what parts of our digitally collated lives seem relevant. Memory may be a fundamental part of cognition, but the next step beyond that is intentionality. It's one thing for AI to remember everything we do, but another for it to decide which information is important to us later. (Ashworth 2024)

Who runs the AI memory machine? There is certainly a new war on memory with digital platforms and algorithms wielding power without accountability, in their supreme capacity to determine what is searchable, censored or erased. Are these the new guardians of remembrance? This is a digital turn on what Viet Thanh Nguyen (2017) calls the 'industry of memory'.

In his superb work, Nguyen argues that the American industry of memory has globally dominated how the Vietnam War has come to be remembered. This industry of memory is much more than any 'memory industry' (for instance the 'professionalization of memory' through museums, archives, history, film, and so on). Rather, 'an industry of memory includes the material and ideological forces that determine how and why memories are produced and circulated, and who has access to, and control of, the memory industries' (2017, 107). In the contemporary era, it is increasingly access to and control over the memory machine, the apps, platforms, devices and services, that enable our capturing, sharing and re-generation of data and information, about ourselves and experiences, that determine how we are known or not, how we are remembered or not. In this way, the memory machine is driven by the new AI industry of memory.

Who then uses, controls, and exploits, and to what ends, the self-produced museum of the real? For us, this is the most urgent question about memory of our times. The answer in part is the new digital and AI industry of memory. This industry includes social media platforms, digital service and app designers and owners, advertisers, data brokers, and all those who make use of the tsunami of content and data that we now routinely and continually produce and share.

This is an industry that reflects the technological and ideological shifts of the internet period. Since the Thatcher and Reagan governments of the 1970s, the dominant global form of capitalism has been neoliberalism, an ideology wherein market logic is applied to all areas of life (Harvey 2007, 23), and 'every social relationship [is] commodified and monetised' (Gilbert 2020, 28). This profit imperative is so dominant over other means of social development that, over time, it has reached hegemonic status, so while market logic does not work in the interests of the vast majority of ordinary people, it has 'become incorporated into the commonsense way we interpret, live in, and understand the world' (Harvey 2007, 23). And the result of this process, 40 or so years on? That society has either forgotten, or given up hope on a world that is not ruled by bankers, and by the new titans of industry, society, and imagination: Big Tech oligarchs (Gilbert 2020, 29, 90, Gilbert & Williams 2022). Just as decades of neoliberalism have left individuals and communities immensely disempowered and alienated from control of their own material circumstances, the same period, by design, has been structured employing our digital embroilment, to shape our pasts, presents, and futures.

Capitalist and colonial societies have a long-established precedent for using data collection and categorisation to construct official narratives and memories that serve political and economic ends (Anderson 1993, 11–15, 2006, 163–185, Cieslik & Margócsy 2022). In the age of AI, and through capitalism's advancing technological front of surveillance and control, we are compelled to consent to a collective myopy (Pilkington 2024). The algorithms we live by offer, paradoxically, endless personalisation, yet limited space for personal reflection and action. In giving up privacy and anonymity in the wholesale resignation of our personal data and human attention, we have exposed and hostaged our memories to the capitalist machine, for access to essential digital services and communication devices and platforms,

Digital empowerment is the empowerment to produce, yet the irony is that this is the basis for the harvesting of the data of the person doing the producing. And what does all your personal data, all those messages, images, and videos from you or depicting you, scattered across the ether, add up to? The answer is: you do not know. In this way, the self is not really known, recognised, or remembered in a traditional humanly graspable sense, but rather unknown, unrecognised, and unremembered, mirror-defying, at least by you and your loved ones.

Instead, the self in the age of algorithms and AI is a commodity, whose conceptualisation and determination is not only beyond our comprehension but also beyond our control. The you that exists in datafied traces of your digital acts and the digital acts of others, be it social media posts, chatbot conversations, or even physical movements silently recorded by your phone's built-in GPS—is fast becoming the most important you in existence. Whether it is the you that determines what content you pour over for hours each day, or the you that AI border technologies decide is or is not worth saving from peril, the datafied self grows in stature and in memory the more data we produce and share.

But with participation in society increasingly contingent on a willingness to forfeit immense volumes of personal data, how can we do anything but support its growth, to consume that which entangles and exposes us, to become ever more memorable by the machine. How will we distinguish the 'real' self from this strange digital one, when life's choices are increasingly mediated by the digital realm, a place we do not own or control, and cannot humanly understand? Your data is not something as simple or recognisable as 'your email address', nor is it something as abstract as 'your privacy'; it is the fuel that powers that thing in your pocket that could once be described as a tool but is now, really, your primary source of information, connection, distraction, dopamine, and memory.

Big Tech now possesses the greatest archive in human history, hoovering up in barely discriminate ways text and images from the internet enabling the creation of words and pictures from human prompts with uncanny results. Large language models (LLMs) scrape vast amounts of data from the so-called publicly available internet. This includes chatbots built on GAI such as Open AI's ChatGPT (ChatGPT 2026), called the fastest growing consumer application in history (Hu 2023). Yet the growth of Big Tech must be situated within the context of capitalism, whose systemic remit is to serve a constant accumulation of capital. Developments in AI therefore cannot be divorced from this imperative. They are not neutral technologies; instead, they both come from and reproduce the structural conditions of the capitalist system. Memory and memory technologies are therefore mediated by this context.

In this ecology, digital connectivity gives memory its new shape, uses, and force, and determines how the past is imagined and imaginable. For example, Brody (1999, 143) argues:

> ... our memory technologies tend to define the very way we metaphorize our lives. Three generations ago, I would likely have categorized every evocative scent as inextricably linked to Proust's

> Madeleines. In my youth, I saw the road to work on an average morning as one long tracking shot in a *Nouvelle Vague* film. Today I find it difficult to think of my life as anything but an interactive net. The connection has become more important than the here and now of the situation.

Brody's words, written at the end of the twentieth century are prescient, for today it is connectivity—to others, to the archive, to the lens of the smartphone itself—which intervenes and interferes with human co-presence, lodged between experience and event. That interference is well documented in psychological studies (see Schacter (2021) for an excellent overview). Today, anticipation and desire for the moment of connectivity, further entangles us with the memory machine.

The digital dopamine hit is not only released through the actual revealed content (reward) of the message, snap, image, video, email, and so on, but even to a greater extent through the anticipation of that content generated through its delivery and potential for delivery. Thus, Greenfield (2021, 38) describes this as 'The maybe factor—the expectation of a possible reward: Who's texting me? Who tagged me on social media? What is in this email?' And as we become increasingly dependent on notifying pings and spiralling algorithmic rabbit holes for cognitive, emotional, and intellectual prompts, the process through which we make sense of the world, and ourselves, is one that is shaped by the fragmenting of algorithmic life. This is why the smartphone is so central to what will become of the past, as it is the supreme vehicle for continuously creating such expectations and relatedly is the primary means of the individual and personal connection to the increasingly lucrative and influential industry of memory. In short, digital nudges nudge memory.

The algorithmic and the personal

Contemporary approaches to memory tend to treat human remembering as an active process, with the accumulation and sifting of thoughts, experiences, events, then represented (including to oneself) and reshaped in the present for present needs. It is then the context of the recall, the purpose of memory in the present (Middleton & Brown 2005, Schacter 1996, Wertsch 2002) that is significant. This also includes forgetting. For example, we can try to repress, change or simply not represent, and forget, difficult or painful experiences. This view of memory as the 'making active' of the past in the present is often traced back to the writing of Bartlett (1932) (see Brown & Hoskins (2010) for a discussion of Bartlett's ideas in relation to media).

However, the digital feed upends this view of remembering, namely as something that is principally humanly shaped, despite being contentious and subject to a range of political and social biases. Today, the present and past are algorithmically but also personally reconstituted through a frenzied and compulsive digital production of the self (recording, emojiing, messaging, sharing, clicking, scrolling). The individual, through a conscious and unconscious digital existence, continually sheds and scatters fragments of itself which are never quite lost as such, but which loiter to haunt our future. Just think of the idea that we are 'followed' around the internet, based on our earlier digital acts and purchases, and even by those of others. But who is following us? And for what purpose?

For instance, Lauren Goode in an illuminating essay for *Wired* explains how despite calling off her wedding, her entanglement in photo apps, cookies, trackers, and algorithms, meant she was 'forever getting married':

> For months, photos of my ex appeared on the Google Home Hub next to my bed, the widgets on my iPad, and the tiny screen of my Apple Watch. So yeah: My ex's face sometimes shows up on my wrist. As I write this, Facebook reminds me that nine years ago I visited him in Massachusetts and met his family's dog. (Goode 2021)

Goode's account reveals how we are embedded in a complex and irresistible digital ecology, that ensnares and collates our identities, experiences, and relationships, through which the past is rendered and retained. We do not realise the impossibility of forgetting and of being forgotten in the *memory feed*, until we try to resist or escape it.

The memory feed (the subject of Chapter 3) is how apps, platforms, and services nudge and compel us to (over)produce data about ourselves and our experiences—which in turn is used to know us, to nudge us, and to remember us—in more powerful and less visible ways. This feed reconstitutes the self as something algorithmically determined, by alienating us from human processes of conceiving memories and controlling their meanings. This means that it empowers those whose interests and objectives are woven into the fabric of the algorithm. At the level of the individual, Elon Musk provides a flagrant example. It was reported that Musk tweaked the X (Twitter) algorithm to boost engagement with his own posts, due to jealousy over US President Joe Biden trending more than him (Schiffer 2024) and as a means of artificially promoting pro-Donald Trump content ahead of the 2024 US presidential election (Cuthbertson 2024). This is evidence of algorithmic platforms as sites of elite distortion. On a structural, insidious level, platforms, or 'mechanisms', 'are better understood as algorithmic decision systems, involving human and computational elements that circumvent the difficulties of modelling human cognition to produce outcomes in services or corporate and industrial interests' (Viljoen, Goldenfein & McGuigan 2021,11). When you remember through the feed, your memory has a commercial purpose. Digital participation is free R&D for the forces with a commercial and political stake in holding your attention.

Given the amount of data sources algorithms and AI draw from, one might expect a degree of neutrality or objectivity in their outputs. But for this to be the case, the systemic drivers that give data sources their value and prestige would need to be neutral too, and so would the powerful actors whose commercial and political interest in Big Tech demands that it is profitable above all else. How can we expect a machine to generate neutral outputs when all its inputs have been biased? As Achiume highlights: 'Technology and its development cannot be divorced from historical structures of oppression, labour exploitation, and various forms of imperialism, including settler colonialism'. Inadequate as a solution to global crises due to its role in reproducing them, the technological innovations of capitalism, 'neither neutral nor objective', are implemented to serve its ends (Achiume, in Molnar 2024b, xiii). Thus, while the memory feed creates obscurity and complexity for some, its rendering of the past is a rich, commodifiable asset for others.

The context of recall, the new context in which we see the world and the world sees us, has a digital dimension. Not only are our previous perceptions, experiences, and memories, re-activated through the incoming stimuli of the present, but they are also algorithmically charged. Thus, as Cheney-Lippold (2017, 26) puts it, 'What the world looks like to you today, and who you are seen to be this afternoon, is constructed from the datafied scraps of what you did last night'.

These two key modes of perception then—how we see the world and how the world sees us, how we remember and how we are remembered—are collapsed through the memory feed. The more we produce media content of ourselves, the more our memories and others' memories of us are shaped and reshaped by opaque algorithms, whose objectives we may not necessarily share or benefit from.

These individualised pasts now circulate, intertwine, connect, and disconnect with others in unknowable ways. We can no longer define and arrest an autobiographical memory, a confident vision of our life trajectory, as our past is something that runs away from us through all our clicks and swipes in the memory feed, to be amassed and given character by an artificial rendering that is beyond our comprehension and control. For vulnerable members of society, such as migrants, on whom decisions are more frequently made than choices are given, this amounts to a significant loss of control over past, present, and future.

Our work

In this book, we can only provide a glimpse of the trajectories of memory of the overproduced and algorithmically distorted self in the memory feed.

Our approach is informed by a series of in-depth interviews from 2021 to 2025 we undertook with some key figures in the industry of memory, namely memory app and service designers and the CEOs of those companies, as well as other experts associated with this field. These services are designed to manage individual and shared photos, videos and other media content, often promoted to ensure that we do not lose precious memories amidst the digital tsunami of our lives. Crucially, they also involve now-pervasive memory prompts through which individuals are routinely confronted with an image, set of photographs, or video that is algorithmically produced from an individual's own collection.

The ways through which your own past can be aggregated and represented to you and to others are increasingly sophisticated. For example, *1 Second Everyday* is an app that takes one second of video every day and then mashes them all together to produce a movie of all these moments rolled into less than a minute at the end of a month or a few minutes at the end of a year. These videos can then be shared in a myriad of ways. *1 Second Everyday* solves the problem or at least meets the need of the overproduction of the self. Most of the accumulating mass of images and video that we continually record will just never be looked at again, because it is beyond human timescales. It thus makes the personal archive meaningful and manageable.

Instead of being satisfied with experiencing an event in the present, we feel compelled to take out our phones and photograph it for future reflection of the past, and we do this so often that our bloated camera rolls include hurried photographs we will probably never choose to look at, their memory only given structure by an app like *1 Second Everyday*. The present is outsourced to the future, the past is outsourced to the smartphone, and memory is outsourced to a memory app.

Our interviews with experts in the industry of memory support a theoretical and conceptual analysis of how memory technologies and indeed wider algorithmic processes of data capture contribute to what we are calling the AI memory machine, a paradoxical set of social and technological conditions for memory, guided by the framework of capitalism.

Our empirical work is not intended to offer some kind of representative sample from which to generalise claims. Rather, we used it to probe and inform debate and argument as to the salient issues around the emergence and effects of the memory feed. Furthermore, the new industry of memory and indeed the wider digital ecology of social media, algorithms, and AI is revolutionary, requiring accounting for capitalism's latest stage of technological development on and exploitation of what memory is and what memory does.

We thus tackle these machinic and human transformations through engaging in interdisciplinary sociological and human science approaches to memory studies, developing from Barnier and Hoskins' (2018) vision of memory 'in the head' and 'in the wild'. As the new memory machine messes with the traditional cognitive and social forces and boundaries of remembering, is the past already lost somewhere in the black box? Or does it give new hope in the revelationary potential of what can now be found?

2
Making of the AI Memory Machine

Introducing the machine

Here, we offer an explanation as to the nature and purpose of the AI memory machine, that individualises and personalises, yet which also massifies and commodifies, memory today. Where does the commercial interest in memory come from, and where might it lead us? How do new artificial, algorithmic, digital technologies differ from past tools, which helped capture, store, and cultivate memory?

Remembering is an achievement in and of a world of individuals and groups encountering, interacting, and colliding with others, objects, institutions, media, political, ideological, and economic systems, and through an array of interfaces, in a situated, ongoing, and yet preempted fashion. Our consciousness, our capacity to remember and to give memories meaning, is shaped by the social world. Memory, often taken as some kind of property or representation of the past, is in fact something that never stops from being altered by the incoming present, and which is never complete. It involves recollection, yet the meaning of this recollection, its framing and its impact, its emergence from the sifting process determining what ends up being forgotten, is a product of present conditions.

Remembering is therefore predisposed, in that it refers to and builds on the past, and yet it is situated in its formation or articulation in the here and now. Today, this here and now in which the individual or group that is remembering and the remembered are inevitably located, is an environment in which the machinic has ever more presence, entanglement with and influence over the human. This is the digital *memory ecology* (Brown & Hoskins 2010, Hoskins & Tulloch 2016), where memories are principally born out of and contingent on the mediatised and hyper-connected social reality of the digital and artificial era.

The AI Memory Machine. Andrew Hoskins, Kristína Čimová, and Danny Pilkington,
Oxford University Press. © Andrew Hoskins, Kristína Čimová, and Danny Pilkington (2026).
DOI: 10.1093/oso/9780198995906.003.0002

The idea of an ecology is often seen as the dynamic relations between organisms and their environment and dated to Haeckel's 1866 work. *Media ecology* is a concept with a rich history in the Toronto School of media theory and in the wider field of media studies (McLuhan 1964, Fuller 2007, Merrin 2014). This has its early glimmerings in Mumford's (1934) *Technics and Civilisation* (above) with his emphasis on the interaction between technological innovation and social life. Merrin (2014, 45) shows, that whereas it is in McLuhan's work where the broad principles of this approach were developed, it was Neil Postman who afforded it form and structure as an academic field. For Postman (1970, 161), 'media ecology is the study of media as environments'. Thus, media ecology 'tries to find out what roles media force us to play, how media structure what we are seeing, why media make us feel and act as we do' (1970, 161).

For us then, the digital memory ecology is today's datafied and mediatised environment in which media force our memorial roles, structure what and how we remember and forget, and make us feel about the past and orient ourselves and our relationships to it. It is the environment wherein decisions are made—by conscious actors and automated processes—about what information is kept and how it is organised and understood. This ecology in the age of the smartphone is always changing and dynamic (hence, it is always new) and, while it is not totally universal, it shapes the remembering and forgetting of billions of individuals.

To implicate the digital memory ecology is to recognise the emergent organic–machinic entwining of remembering and forgetting, at once individual and collective, rather than as siloed, static, or set adrift. Again, memory as part of an ecology is always situated, ongoing, and yet predisposed, bumping up against and being transformed in, the emergent present.

Today, data, social media, and algorithmic technologies are utterly transforming this ecology to the extent that what memory is and what memory does are being revolutionised. Memory is given new forms of both continuity and disruption through the memory feed (introduced in Chapter 1, and the subject of Chapter 3).

At the heart of our approach is to recognise that the systemic forces driving the technological and social conditions structuring and profiting from the digital memory ecology are those of capital and capitalism. Although it seems we are living through a period of unprecedented and rapid technological revolution, digital and AI machinic motivations are already traceable to the history of capitalist and colonial technological innovation. Their primary purpose—capital accumulation—is unchanged, albeit data has become a dominant form of capital in and of itself, with the internet providing its owners with novel means of social control (Walton & Nayak 2021, 1). These broad methods, where informational capital is identified and preserved through tactical surveillance and control, have deep historical roots.

Four decades into a neoliberal dismantling of the institutions that confer social and democratic power, and the class consciousness required to utilise it, society has been rendered newly vulnerable to capitalism's advancing mechanisms of surveillance and control: data, social media, and artificial intelligence. The emergent risk here is a myopic trajectory, where systemically diminished agency over both our material conditions and our memory-making processes is putting constraints on the parameters of class consciousness and political imagination (Pilkington 2024).

But how did we get here? And how is capitalist memory-making any different now than before the age of AI?

The politics of externalising memory

There is a long history of an 'external' memory field of media, with cave art from Sulawesi, Indonesia, being dated at almost 40,000 years old. And each stage of externalisation through the media of memory: oral–written–printed–electronic (Donald 2002, Hoskins 2017) transformed what was possible for the mind to represent, re-visit, store, hold, manage, understand, and remember. Yet, this massive expansion of the human capacity for memory has not necessarily expanded the social rights of those being remembered. Just as memory's capacity has grown, so has its commercial and political value. The exploitation of externalised memory-making through technological innovation traces a clear path through the history of capitalism (Pilkington 2024).

While external forms of memory have long existed, it has been during the capitalist period that they have found a renewed purpose in defining not only the past but also the present and future. Prior to capitalism, the public record was quite limited. In the UK, for example, it was not until 1538 that Parishes were first decreed to record basic information such as baptisms, marriages, and deaths, with gravestones adding further data points such as dates of birth and familial relationships.[1] In 1086, King William I's (the Conqueror) Domesday Book asked fixed questions about who lived where in his Kingdom and what land they owned as a way to work out how much tax he could charge them (The National Archives 2025); but the first proper census, taken in 1801, asked about the type of work people were involved in, with more and more employment categories added in the years that followed (Office for National Statistics 2022).

While the Domesday Book is evidence of the long history of the state mapping out its land and subjects for the purposes of taxation, the introduction and development of censuses showed how the state was gaining interest in recording and categorising more and more.[2] Such a process, ostensibly for the purposes of resource allocation and future planning, also represented a site of struggle between disenfranchised groups and the state. Protesting for the right to vote, the Suffragettes campaigned for women to boycott the 1911 census, refusing to be counted by a government that they could not elect. Objections were also raised about new questions in the census asking women about the length of their marriage and the number of children they had (Office for National Statistics 2022). Not only was the principle being challenged, that one should give over information to a state whose institutions upheld inequality, the instrument itself was being called into question for its role in reinforcing such inequalities. It is worth mentioning that the census has been a site of struggle right up to the present day, with Muslim groups successfully lobbying for the *addition* of a question on religion in 2001 because previous ethnic categorisations failed to statistically capture the levels of disadvantage experienced by Muslim communities. Hussain (2025) describes how Muslim organisations wanted the census to better reflect their experience of inequality, hoping this might lead towards a fairer allocation of resources, whereas many Muslims were apprehensive to participate at all; they feared that normalised Islamophobia could see statistics being misconstrued, and they were doubtful that the state would actually use the data to benefit Muslim communities. Such tensions illustrate the bargaining that goes into data collection between those in and out of power:

If we know more, we can help you more.

Ok, but why aren't you helping me now anyway?

It is no accident that this transition towards increasing the public record occurred at a time when capitalism was transforming feudal relations of service into permanent relations of wage labour (Graeber 2018). These relations premised that society would be geared towards the accumulation of profit for those who owned resources, because of the exploitation of those who owned only their labour power. The latter group, a new proletarian working class, had to be managed: 'the new bureaucratically organised corporations and their "scientific management" sought as far as possible to literally turn workers into extensions of the machinery, their every move predetermined by someone else' (Graeber 2018, 226, 233).

With life subsumed in this process of exploitation, a process wherein the value of a resource (read: person) is extracted and unequally shared, new importance was placed on using externalised memory as a tool for categorising social life and thus optimising it for commodification and control. The oversight is not necessarily the source of tension, but rather, the form of governance this oversight serves is one of exploitation.

Benedict Anderson in *Imagined Communities*, his seminal study of nationalism, highlights this process using the example of European colonialism in South-East Asia. Through mapmaking, museum-curation, and census records, colonial states externalised a highly politicised version of history. With these tools, the colonial state was able to profoundly shape 'the way in which [it] imagined its dominion—the nature of the human beings it ruled, the geography of its domain, and the legitimacy of its ancestry' (Anderson 2006, 163–164). In mid-nineteenth-century British-colonial Malaya, the subjugated Malay people would be 'continuously agglomerated, disaggregated, recombined, intermixed, and reordered' through census records (Anderson 2006, 163–164). The Dutch colony of Indonesia developed a census where racial distinctions superseded established forms of rank. This had a profound impact on the agency and rights of subjugated people, whose census categorisation determined how they 'dress, reside, marry, be buried, and bequeath property' (Anderson 2006, 168).

Colonial structures have also been shaped with maps, drawn and applied to perpetuate colonial dominance and surveillance, letting people living (back home) in the colonising country know the areas of the world 'they' had influence in, despite having never been there themselves. European populations could therefore remember the parameters of the world in colonial terms and imagine the future of the world and their place in it (Anderson 2006, 176). This national identity, proudly embraced, perpetuated through a shared understanding of colonial triumph, enmeshed visions of national interest with the commercial interest of those in power—The Dutch United East India Company was instrumental in the establishment of Dutch colonies in the East Indies (Anderson 2006), indeed, just as the United Fruit Company was instrumental in the United States' imperial ventures in late twentieth-century Central America (Prashad 2020). In this sense, the capitalist colonial period marked the beginning of a new era for externalised, recorded memory, one where memory itself was a form of capital, a space, there, vulnerable, and ripe for colonisation. Just as commercial interests would shape colonial institutions and identities, they would have a role in the production of memory.

For colonised people, the system of oppression endured was legitimised through lavish and revisionist monuments built on their land, the same plundered and impoverished land on which they lived suffered lives, to 'remind' them that they 'have always been, or have long become, incapable of either greatness or self-rule' (Anderson 2006, 181). Having the financial and legislative capacity to physically construct history in the form of monuments and museums meant that colonial powers could assert authority over memory and, importantly, its enduring impact on public life.

Furthermore, the significant scale of data collection (through censuses and record-keeping) was novel at the time. Subjugated populations, happy or unhappy in their lives, while aware of the antagonistic relationship with their oppressor, may have had no idea of the extent to which they were 'being mapped from on high' (Anderson 2006, 168). There is an obvious parallel here with the way AI technologies accumulate data about us and run it through an algorithm to determine who we are, what we might have done, and what we might do next (Viljoen, Goldenfein & McGuigan 2021, 6, 8).

Indeed, Anderson's analysis of the instruments of nineteenth-century colonialism has much to tell us about capitalism's instruments of control today. Colonial states, enabled by technological tools (then: print, but now: AI) harnessed towards political and economic objectives, 'did not merely aspire to create, under [their] control, a human landscape of perfect visibility; the condition of this "visibility" was that everyone, everything, had (as it were) a serial number' (Anderson 2006, 184–185). This is a process of dehumanisation that varies in outcome.

Israel's colonial occupation of Palestine and genocidal campaign in Gaza (see news and press releases in United Nations 2022 and United Nations Human Rights 2025) provides a nightmarish example. AI-powered Automated Target Recognition (ATR) technologies, deployed to identify or generate targets for bombing, have resulted in the deaths of thousands of Palestinian civilians (Abraham 2024). Rationalising patterns in historical data, the 'widespread use of algorithmically induced targets is designed to project threat, ad infinitum, into the (un)forseeable future' (Downey 2025, 15); AI ascribes a meaning to the past that satisfies the needs of Israel's present 'political imperative of wholesale destruction' (Downey 2025, 11).

So, while AI technologies present novel challenges, many of their features are not necessarily new. Nor are the motivations behind their implementation (profit accumulation, political power) and their beneficiaries (the ruling class, those in power). Cieslik and Margócsy (2022, 353) propose that 'datafication' is 'not a one-time result of a technological invention', but rather,

> European states have relied on large-scale data sets for managing their colonies at least since 1500, and they never failed to provide utopian narratives that claimed these efforts would bring tangible benefits to the populations affected. History has seen again and again how governments and agencies resort to the large-scale collection of data (including data on the private lives of people) and their mathematical analysis to drive development. Arguably, the persistent decoupling of colonial datafication and recent datafication processes is both deliberate and political. Positioning current datafication as a new and original phenomenon comes with a promise of a positive, technology-driven social change. (Cieslik and Margócsy 2022, 368)

The 'perfect visibility' described by Anderson is integral to the business models of digital advertisement companies such as Google and Facebook, who use algorithms to track our locations, clicks, and even cognitive states, to profile our probabilities as consumers (Viljoen, Goldenfein & McGuigan 2021, 8). The scale of surveillance in the age of AI easily reaches the intimate everyday, not least with the continuity of connectivity of smart devices.

Companies like Meta, for example, state: 'We understand that sometimes ads can be so specific, it seems like we must be listening to your conversations through your microphone, but we're not' (Griffin 2024). But this is hardly reassuring, given as it hints at just how acutely we are being tracked in a myriad of other unknown ways. The related advances of internet, social media, and smartphone, mark a new phase of media's externalisation of memory, through the recording and mining of the minutiae of life. At the same time, these mess up the relationship between memory in the head and in the wild, obscuring the proprietors and the provenance of the past.

Whereas social media once seemed an innocent tool for sharing the goings-on of and in the present, it has become an astonishing and unfathomable archive, from which the past is being mined—and lost—anew. Apps and services help manage and seemingly secure the flow of the memory feed, and yet, at the same time, render the past untameable. With ever-deepening layers of complexity, and instant access, the lines between past and present are becoming increasingly blurred; the very concept of time is contested (Jungselius & Weilenmann 2023, 13).

The memory machine—through algorithmic, datafied, virtual worlds and the superficial agency we possess in them—reinvents the past in how it is rendered present, durable and meaningful, or lost, hidden or obscured. It makes its origins, trajectories, and ultimately its human provenance, fuzzy. For instance, Brown et al. (2024) usefully consider that obfuscation on the level of algorithmic advertising, based on a complex interplay between ad and user built up over time, is tuned not necessarily to things we recognise in ourselves but rather to a *vibe* we are immersed in through heavily tracked online engagement. This vibe is a response to an identity co-created by us and with the advertisements we engage with online; it is a commercial product and by extension, a new self, opaque and difficult to trace back to an original starting point in our own wants, needs, and identities, in emergent digital everydays.

The paradox of digital advertising is that while each of us experiences its algorithmic flow as an intimate and persistent rhythm in our lives, that flow is no longer a public cultural form open to the kinds of mass criticism, appreciation, and analysis that gave us a shared understanding of advertising—and associated forms of accountability—in the broadcast media era (Brown et al. 2024, 13–14).

Where traditional advertising was open to contestation, the interests of marketers and consumers are more distinct. Algorithmic advertising, is more difficult to pin down because these interests have been obfuscated by intense personalisation. There is no 'us' and 'them', only 'you'; and you are a product of the vibes generated by your behaviour in the digitised commercial sphere. This creates a paradox of the self. The self that the machine remembers through data is of great commercial value, therefore it is exploited. The you that comprises everything you have ever posted, clicked, and read online, and is made sense of by an algorithm designed to make commercial and/or political decisions about this you, is of detail beyond human comprehension, while for the machine designed to understand it, it is a subject of manipulation.

However, in the real world, where we experience that exploitation materially, participation in society is contingent on feeding the machine large volumes of data that make us ever more vulnerable and exploitable.

The 'gains in wealth and power derived from data mining far outweigh the agency gained by the average user' (Timcke 2021, 29). This is the great, disempowering paradox. In the current state of play, our relationship to memory is like many other individual and social phenomena in that it is not somehow recoverable or retrievable to the state it once was before the connective turn (above).

Remembering through connectivity

Some cognitive scientists and philosophers argue that cognition is not something bound by the head (or even the body) but extended and distributed across our social worlds. Influential then is the 'extended mind' thesis (Clark 2008, Menary 2010), which John Sutton defines as the idea that 'mental states and processes can spread across the physical, social, and cultural environments as well as bodies and brains' (2005, 223). Important in this work around distributed cognition is the idea of 'return', in that human remembering is a kind of loop or circuit out from the head and into the wild and then back again (Clark 2008, 77). The functions of the mind and of remembering are thus strengthened by their reaching out for support from external mechanisms, including media and other people, who help 'scaffold' (Sutton 2008) our memories. And underpinning the establishment of the concept of 'collective memory', is that without social scaffolds or frameworks our memories would not materialise or become meaningful (Halbwachs 1980).

But the contemporary transformation is of individuals' remembering being not only dependent upon external worlds into which the loops or extensions of the human mind travel, but that the digital memory ecology is constructed through new loops and extensions—entire infrastructures of unimaginable complexity and scale—through which memories are remade, managed, as well as hidden, lost, and erased. One of the most illustrative examples of this kind of infrastructure is social media. These are landscapes of intense informational war, where algorithmic hierarchies reward engagement, rather than credibility.

In the maelstrom, fake news rapidly proliferates alongside truth, and it can be difficult to distinguish between the two. Yet even when we can, this does not necessarily mean that we will remember making such distinctions in the future. Instead, at the times of recall, memories have been further conditioned by their cognitive and social worlds, which are increasingly digitally afforded and shaped. In these circumstance, it becomes difficult to remember the source of information, especially 'peripheral' aspects that we may not have even consciously registered at the time (Levy 2017, 29). In the swirling cauldron of the digital memory ecology, provenance is muddied, realities are sharded.

Once we could identify more centrally the individual as a fundamental agent in the remembering and forgetting of themselves and their social worlds, albeit assisted and influenced, enabled and constrained, by external others, mechanisms and media. But today, this relationship is thrown into reverse. It is us who are known and remembered, not only through but also *by* digital technologies and algorithms (whose depiction of us is a rich commodity). This is then not only a matter of our new outsourced dependency on tech for remembering, that is how we remember *this* or *that*, but through our dependency, the machine is able to remember *us*. The remembering subject is transformed overnight into the remembered object. On the one hand, we see our devices as innovative and convenient tools for helping us remember things. Yet, as Ashworth (2024) puts it: 'Your phone is already siphoning off all the data it can get from you, from your location to your grocery shopping habits to which Instagram accounts you double tap the most'. This is the memory feed; it is we who feed the machine.

With the smartphone, the internal and external, here and there, now and then, private and public traditional boundaries of remembering and forgetting are elided into a highly connected and continuous digital memory ecology. The smartphonc, in its constant presence, its continuity of signals, its anticipation of connectivity, rewires the self so that memory becomes something pulled in with the digital desire for attention and contact. As Serafinelli (2020, 7, cited in Jungselius & Weilenmann 2023) puts it, 'sharing photos becomes synonymous with keeping memories alive'.

What happens here is not only a fusion of communication with the archive (all our digital communicational acts are archival in terms of the digital traces produced), but also the past—and expressly *your* past—is used and entangled in the digital desire for and anticipation of contact. Put simply, memory becomes less a process for understanding, and increasingly a means of securing another dopamine hit.

This is not to suggest that memory stops once that immediate dopamine hit wears off. The algorithms on your various smartphone applications and platforms nudge your past into view, constantly seducing you to click on it and smile or cry again. 'Take a look at you!' your phone screams, presenting its latest curation of your memories, with the algorithm delivering your past sampled and arranged (including to music) based on the metamemory of you—your snapping, uploading, viewing, liking, and sharing habits. Indeed, even when these nudges take the form of advertisements and suggested social media content, they are ostensibly created because of the accumulating history of your previous digital engagements. What could be more personal than the past you have already made? The smartphone is the ultimate memory machine, as it constantly confronts the user with their self and a memory of their self. But who or what exactly is remembering you and your past, and for what purpose?

Dehumanising society

To address this question, on the purpose of the memory machine, we return briefly to Achiume: 'Technology and its development cannot be divorced from historical structures ... [therefore it is] neither neutral nor objective' (Achiume in Molnar 2024b, xiii). How can we assess the merits and limitations of technology without understanding the relationship of interests between the factors driving and funding its innovation, and the outcomes of its implementation? How can we properly make sense of our present juncture and where might we be heading next if we overlook the reasons we got here in the first place?

As we have highlighted, the machinic transformation occurring in human memory is fundamentally an outcome of capitalism's imperative to colonise and incorporate all aspects of human and social life towards capital accumulation. This has been an evolving process of dehumanisation, and in the age of neoliberalism and AI, what we understand as human memory has sustained a lethal blow. To fully explore why the past is all over, we must understand the technologies and relations that produce a certain past in the first place.

It is impossible to divorce the technological innovations of the capitalist period from the capitalist context from which they were born, conceived, funded, and applied. In Ernest Mandel's (1990) introduction to Karl Marx's *Capital*, he lays out the fundamental basis of this context, that 'the basic drive of the capitalist mode of production is the drive to accumulate capital'. This primary objective is systemic rather than a simple product of the personal inclinations of capitalists; the *system* is predicated on competition between accumulating capitals. Without this competition, economic growth stagnates, and monopolies undermine the competitive basis of capitalism. Yet, in 1917, Lenin (2021 [1917]) described monopolisation as an inevitable outcome of capitalism: '... the rise of monopolies, as the result of the concentration of production, is a general and fundamental law of the present stage of development of capitalism'.

It remains so today, and we are reminded of this every time we order a packet of screws through Amazon because it is cheaper and more convenient than walking round to the local hardware store. The Big Tech monopolisation of AI technology is no different. Indeed, in 2024, the United States' trade regulating body, the Federal Trade Commission (FTC) opened an investigation into Microsoft, Amazon, and Google over potential breaches in competition rules arising from their vast investments in the field of AI (Montgomery & Paul 2024). Competition is fierce among the monopolists; financial investment must yield financial returns. Data is now arguably the number one commodity; the primary control mechanism through which capitalism asserts its systemic objective: that 'profit rules over people' (Walton & Nayak 2021, 1). This means that our memory, or more so, the memory of us, is a rich source of fuel for the machine.

It is not simply the case that evil capitalist overlords sit rubbing their hands together thinking of ways to extract more profit at our expense (although they do exist and may well do that!), but rather, that the system itself is entirely predicated upon a relentless, creative (yet somewhat predictable), and competitive money-making pursuit. It would fall apart without it. The system drives the motivations of these actors, and they as its beneficiaries in turn drive the system, inflicting it upon ordinary people without sharing its rewards.

Yet this integral—if perhaps doomed—system of competition corresponds to another force weighted towards the sole objective of securing profits: the use and expansion of 'labour-saving devices'. If everyone was employed and wages correspondingly rose at the expense of profits, then capitalist economic growth would diminish and ultimately vanish (Mandel in Marx 1990, 60). To follow this process to its logical conclusion, is a scenario where first machines do everything, and then eventually, one machine, owned by one monopolistically dominant proprietor—the only human left—does everything. But let us take a few steps back and focus on our present dilemma, the context of which Mandel importantly addresses:

> Because capital accumulation presupposes production for profit, because it has profit maximisation as its very *rationale*, exact and minute cost calculations entail constant reorganisations of the production process with the single purpose of reducing costs .... Capitalist economy is thus a gigantic enterprise of dehumanisation, of transformation of human beings from goals in themselves into instruments and means for money-making and capital accumulation. It is not the machine, nor any technological compulsion, which inevitably transforms workers and men and women in general into appendices and slaves of monstrous equipment. It is the capitalist principle of profit maximisation by individual firms which unleashes this terrifying trend. Other types of technology and other types of machine are perfectly conceivable – provided that the guiding principle of investment is no longer 'cost saving' by individual competing firms, but the optimum development of all human beings. (Mandel 1990, 65)

Mandel originally wrote this in 1976, and Karl Marx published the first volume of *Capital* in 1867, but the process described is one that defines our relationship with technology today. The dehumanisation being described does not only refer to machines replacing us in the field of production (Walton & Nayak 2021), but additionally, the machinic logic of capital accumulation subsuming all aspects of our consciousness. Memory is shackled to this reality, its human and autonomous elements subsumed within its structure. Timcke (2021, 3–4) proposes that capitalism has embedded itself within cultural and technological development to the point that a 'great simplification of the world' has occurred, where no alternative to capitalism is possible and the system of capitalism is able to abstract itself from the horrors it produces. Human life is simplified along lines of profitability and nothing else. In the twenty-first century, this dehumanisation takes the form of *datafication*:

> Datafication is a process which converts human practices into computational artefacts. It also involves the advocacy for and implementation of computational reason to oversee human life ... capitalism has a code that constitutes society. When adhering to this code, datafication encompasses a transformation of the grand tapestry of human life to quantifiable bits to then be computed for profit-seeking activities. (Timcke 2021, 3–4)

Following Timcke, the 'computational reason' overseeing human life and the computational resources required to implement it have not only been captured but '*flattened* to satisfy the requirements of a capitalist ruling class' (Timcke 2021, 3–4). This has had profound negative consequences for human agency. In an illuminating conversation about the trajectory of feminism in the neoliberal era, Banet-Weiser, Gill, and Rottenberg note that the datafied context of platform capitalism presents a paradoxical roadblock for those who wish to challenge capitalist hegemony. On the one hand, the feedback loop of the media context popularises that which is most visible, yet on the other, as 'most circuits of visibility are driven by profit', by thc timc a message is popularised it will have been commercialised, emptied, its original meaning entirely flattened out (2019, 12). Thus, not only does capitalism absorb and smooth out our expressions of dissent, it rewards, with popularity, the blunted commercial realities created instead.

With memory increasingly dependent on digital and AI environments for survival, what chance does it stand but to have its sting removed, its originality and human authenticity curbed, its relation to the real human being at its source all but gone. For anyone who sees technology as humanity's great saviour, a benevolent and apolitical force able to transcend the constraints of politics and economics and deliver us to a new promised land, this Marxist interpretation might seem wildly misguided. Yet as we will show, technology is not divorceable from the system that produced it.

Superintelligent capitalism

Big Tech business is booming. Of the top ten figures on Forbes' magazine's 2024 'billionaire list' (Forbes 2024), eight are or have been senior figures in Twitter, Facebook, Amazon, Google, Oracle, or Microsoft. From a legislative perspective, governments are grappling with their role in facilitating the dominance of Big Tech and responsibility to regulate in some way that preserves profits yet prevents disruption (Molnar 2023). In the digital ecology, truth-seeking processes, memory, fact, and reality have all been blown wide open to new interpretation and condemnation (Happer 2024). Generative AI (GAI), with its relatively unknown potential or at least limits, is a fast emergent driver of the new landscape of scepticism, excitement, and uncertainty.

Large Language Models such as Open AI's Chat GPT, DALL-E, Google's Gemini (formerly Bard), and Stable Diffusion are programmes which, given a textual prompt, can generate 'new' output based on the trillions of eventualities they have learnt about by combing through available internet data, from books to social media posts (Mearian 2024). This generative capacity, with its seemingly infinite potential, has raised questions around the extent to which AI can or will be able to perform and outperform human agents in processes of learning and production. This manifests primarily in two ways: (1) fear/hope that humans will be replaced in the field of production, and (2) fear/hope that humans will be replaced as a species. We lay out some of the core arguments from these perspectives and our analysis of them below.

1. AI is going to take/do our jobs

This first point partially concerns the matter of whether GAI is creating new artefacts or simply imitating existing ones, and the implications this has for perceptions of authenticity and the value of artefacts created by human beings (Magni, Park & Manchi 2023, Yiu, Kosoy & Gopnik 2023, Clarke 2022). In the creative industries, there is a fear that human-made art risks being devalued by AI imitations, which sparks debate over who or what gets to define something as authentic to begin with. In other industries—most human workplaces—the concern is whether AI can outright do or replace the job of a human therefore render human workforces obsolete and unemployed. However, it is also argued that people overestimate the impact of AI on administrative and managerial jobs, with certain functions in care work and culture production so heavily reliant on human connection, relatability, and persona, that AI poses little risk (Brentler 2024).

Whichever position one takes on how this looks in the future, there are some material realities to consider now. The beginning of the digital age coincided with the West-driven global lurch towards free-market neoliberalism in and from the 1980s. In that time, as a means of overseeing the replacement of human agency and imagination with the blanket logic of the market (Gilbert & Williams 2022), more and more superfluous administrative and managerial roles have been *created* in place of the genuinely productive ones (such as industry, arts, healthcare, education, etc.) being constantly cut and 'restructured' (Graeber 2018). This suggests a potential outcome for AI whereby middle and upper classes are 'looked after' within obscure and unproductive 'white collar' managerial desk jobs, while the working class (including those in unproductive, bureaucratic administrative roles) suffer job replacement. In any case, the shift appears to be one that heightens capitalism's tendency to measure productivity in terms of how much profit has been produced, replacing human beings in productive roles and therefore dividing them into two socially unproductive groups: those who oversee this charade, and those who are forced to work in service of it.

This point is particularly relevant considering GAI's situation within the context of the capitalist mode of production. There is a view existing across the political spectrum, which centres the potentially liberating aspect of AI, where humans could be freed from the burden of work and afforded a more fruitful existence (Robinson 2023). Others, by contrast, hold that AI under capitalism is already used and could continue to be used to extract rather than redistribute profit, seeing humans further alienated from capital and power (O'Shea 2024, Slater 2021, Milne, Foley & Ramand 2023). This latter perspective has indeed been realised, whether through Uber CEO Dara Khosrowshahi admitting that the company uses algorithmically driven 'behavioural patterns' to determine drivers' pay, a measure that has been described as 'algorithmic wage discrimination' (Wray 2024), or in the 'contemporary tech-enabled surveillance practices' that overpolice the lives of Black people in the USA (Byrum & Benjamin 2022).

Whether AI, based on its technological capabilities alone, *could* liberate ordinary people from current burdens or not is immaterial. The reality is that AI, developed and implemented under capitalism, is already being used to facilitate cost-saving imperatives, not social and economic empowerment. We have little reason to believe this dynamic will change under the present system. It is the system—capitalism—that captures technology's social potential and refocuses it on the pursuit of profit. This is nothing new. When Salvador Allende, a socialist, was democratically elected to the Chilean presidency in 1970, he embraced latent computing technologies to build Cybersyn, an early form of internet that would be used in Chile to allow citizens to connect and participate in democratic economic planning (Gilbert 2020, 100). Unlike the internet now, owned by unaccountable Big Tech elites who use it to interfere in democracy (Momtaz 2025), computing systems under Allende's socialist government some 50 years ago stood to deepen it. Of course, this was an experiment that the capitalist West did not allow to play out. The potential of a successful, futuristic socialist project struck fear into the hearts of Western capitalists whose mass of wealth and power risked being more evenly distributed, so a murderous CIA-backed military coup deposed Allende's government in 1973, replacing it with a new experiment altogether; an ideological one, in the form of neoliberalism (Gilbert 2020, 100, Prashad 2020). Applications of technology since then, in Chile and across the globe, have reflected this ideological shift.

2. AI is going to kill us all

This debate is a highly polarised one. Divergent levels of optimism and scepticism have created opposing camps in the field (Crawford 2021). These include: the 'x-risk' (or 'AI doomer') community, who believe AI poses an existential threat to humanity, with extinction a real prospect; AI ethicists, who are less concerned with potential doomsday scenarios in the future and instead focused on the immediate impact of AI being used irresponsibly by powerful humans and systems (see Milne, Foley & Ramand 2023); and AI boosters, who believe AI should be unregulated and allowed to proliferate because it will solve the world's problems and transcend existing (political and economic) solutions. AI boosterism is associated with 'effective accelerationism' ('e/acc'), the idea that accelerated techno-capitalism and a 'post-human' future is humanity's logical next step (Lovely 2024).

There is a fear that GAI will massively increase misinformation and disinformation, producing fake material so realistic that we struggle to differentiate between what is real and what has been maliciously generated as an act of disruption or distortion (Fried 2023, Hsu & Thompson 2023). With the rise of AI-generated deepfake images (many of which are nonconsensual pornographic content) (Beaumont-Thomas 2024) and AI bots used to impersonate political candidates, 70% of British MPs now fear AI will be used to spread misinformation and disinformation (Milmo 2024) and more than 75% of the British public fear that misinformation and deepfakes will interfere with democratic process in forthcoming elections (Landi 2024).

However, these fears have also been disputed as a contemporary moral panic around the threat of new technologies to humankind (Simon et al. 2023, Levy 2023, Yiu, Kosoy & Gopnik 2023). Indeed, evidence from Israel and Palestine suggests that greater misinformation arises from out-of-context journalistic coverage than GAI-produced fake images (Bedingfield 2023). Furthermore, misinformation and disinformation are already widespread regardless of whether GAI-produced content exists. Algorithms feed off engagement, which makes outrageous content popular, as everyone engages with it whether they agree with it or not. This allows and indeed encourages the misogynistic views of real public figures (like Andrew Tate) to proliferate online and misinform audiences (Weale 2024). Followers of controversial figures watch the content because they agree with it; 'haters' watch the content to reject it. Either way, the algorithm reads the content as popular and therefore worth illuminating further in our feeds, pulling us ever deeper into the digital attention economy.

The measure of AI's threat to humanity is perhaps most deeply contested in the debate around artificial *general* intelligence (AGI). Where previous AI models have been acknowledged for their high level of competence and accuracy in a given domain (for example, an AI solely programmed to be good at chess, and consequently able to beat a human at chess, but not much else), an AGI would be able to solve all problems that humans can, across a range of domains, and even to a better and more efficient standard (Chehreghani 2024, 1, Sublime 2024, 42, Castro & New 2016). To achieve this, an AGI would need to: be *general*, in its ability to engage with a variety of tasks; be *adaptable*; be *creative*; possess *common sense* and the ability to *reason*; have *long term memory*, and even *self-awareness* and *consciousness* (Sublime 2024, 42). Furthermore, possessing this well-rounded intelligence (which until now has been the preserve of the human species alone) and a computerised capacity to elevate this intelligence *above* that of humans—with potentially adverse outcomes for humans—leads to a level of AI now commonly described as 'superintelligence'.

The field of AI is torn over whether AGI and eventual superintelligence are foreboding or enriching prospects (Bengio 2023). Additionally, the scientific, ethical, and political debate around the future risks of AI technology is entangled with the profit-driven motives of AI business. Sam Altman, CEO of OpenAI (the company behind ChatGPT) embodies this contradiction. Altman has publicly questioned the role of profit in driving AI developments (Lovely 2024), and in July 2023, OpenAI launched its 'Superalignment' initiative which aims to 'align' potentially 'superintelligent' AI's with 'human intent ... preventing [the AI] from going rogue' (Leike & Sutskever 2023). The programme demonstrates an ostensible concern with autonomous capabilities of AI in the near future, suggesting these will need reigning in to avoid 'rogue' outcomes.

Memory, it has been said, has already gone rogue, as media and cultural technologies have placed the tools of memory-making outside of the control of the state and into the hands of anyone with access to the internet (De Kosnick 2016, 2). Memory is no longer something defined predominately by state records and the wider memory industry. Instead, the new industry of memory is something much more open to manipulation and reinvention by anyone with access to the tools of generative AI.

It is Big Tech that has most effectively exploited the greatest new resources of memory in history, using it for the purpose of capital accumulation at the expense of our privacy and agency as individuals and as a society. Yet roguish data manipulation, unaligned with human progress, is something Big Tech claims to be worried about. In the months prior to co-founding OpenAI, Altman stated 'AI will probably most likely lead to the end of the world, but in the meantime, there'll be great companies' (Lovely 2024). Having acknowledged in January 2023 that the worst-case scenario for humanity was a 'lights out' situation, he did not mention extinction while under oath before senators a few months later (Lovely 2024). Altman has called for the US Congress to regulate AI, yet OpenAI parent company Microsoft—who have reportedly invested $13bn in the company (Financial Times 2023) prompting the FTC investigation into potential breaches of competition rules we mentioned earlier (Montgomery & Paul 2024)—have lobbied for ChatGPT's exemption from restrictions, and Altman himself has lobbied the EU for less AI regulation (Lovely 2024). Indeed, addressing US lawmakers in 2025, Altman urged that regulations should not slow down the US in its AI race with China (Goldman 2025).

Contradictions such as these render any technology-centric debate about AI, whether it is all hype or horror, as farcical. Nonetheless, somewhat ironically, the broad debate about AI's role in the future of humanity and its systems of governance is always really a debate about the future of capitalism.

'Technofascism' and the neoliberal imagination

Scottish comedian and writer Frankie Boyle's 2022 novel, *Meantime* ponders society's direction of travel at our current, AI-driven juncture. One of the characters, a political activist called Amy, wonders about the similarities between this trajectory and that of preceding periods of fascism: 'my worry is that we might be heading towards some type of techno fascism, although it might be just a type of hyper-surveillance that is indistinguishable from actual fascism: where everyone is reduced to a kind of ultra-monitored husk' (Boyle 2022, 78). The risk identified here is such that surveillance capitalism stands to 'reduce' and hollow out public consciousness to the point of obsolescence—we are reminded here of the capitalist tendency to 'flatten' dissent. But more, the '*indistinguishability*' of 'techno-fascism' from 'actual fascism' speaks to a new dimension of ideological hegemony in the artificial era. Not only is ideology so deeply embedded that its variations and vulgarities shift without contest, but its reach is also made possible by material realities of past and present having been subject to such obfuscation that the root of ideology is no longer understood by the public at all. As we have discussed, part of this comes with a media context that rewards fake news and truth equally; engagement and commercial value trump credibility. But also, our own inability to distinguish and understand the ideological and material implications of the present, is a result of the waning autonomy of individual and social memory in an environment where the character of memory is primarily determined by a (capitalist) algorithm.

In their analysis of emergent 'fake history' on Twitter after the 2021 US Capitol riots, Evans and Rigato (2024) reveal the bizarre tendencies of both Republican and Democrat supporters, who find ways to compare both Biden and Trump to both Stalin and Hitler. New buzzwords and terms that emerge online create analogies 'rooted in the memory and not the actual history of National Socialism' (Evans & Rigato 2024, 181), indicating that warped digital memories carry more significance than the historical basis of competing ideologies. With no need for evidence to support claims, 'The Republican base is willing to wield history as a cudgel as long as it allows them to maintain their sense of victimhood' and similarly, Democrats favour communication that serves primarily as a 'galvanizing force' for 'emotional retaliation' (Evans & Rigato 2024, 185). It is no wonder that US politics, where the two main parties broadly represent the same set of elite interests, is so frequently described as an increasingly polarised battleground. Naturally, with ideologies obscured by buzzwords, and an absence of historical evidence to ballast distorted yet emotionally resonant memories, the debate has become fractured and, in many ways, emptied of meaning.

Resisting this disposition, let us consider the particulars of Frankie Boyle's point on the technofascist character of AI. As indicated above, fascism is a word often unhelpfully bandied around to describe the world's bad guys, who operate from quite different political contexts to those of 1930s Europe. Yet there are some shared characteristics worth noting.

First, capitalism has consistently shown its willingness to lurch to the political right to preserve its material interest in the capitalist system of inequality. The US media heaped praise on Benito Mussolini in the 1920s and early 1930s for saving Italy from communism, and US companies such as General Motors and Ford owned factories in enemy countries that produced 'fuel, tanks, and planes' used to attack Allied forces during the Second World War (Parenti 1997, 5, 19). Fascism should be understood as a product and a preserver of the interests of capitalism rather than its antithesis.

For a contemporary example, the 2025 announcement by Meta Chief Executive Mark Zuckerberg that the company will be relaxing its anti-misinformation fact-checking procedures, as well as its rules around language (which could impact social groups who receive online harassment), is an indication that the tech titans of capitalism are responding to how cosmopolitan social liberalism is on the way out, with figures like Donald Trump, hostile to minority groups, on the way in. Zuckerberg's decision 'positions Meta for the political landscape of the moment, with conservative power ascendant in Washington' (Isaac, Frenkel & Conger 2025). This is a clear indication that the character and tone of capital will shift and align with the ideologies (variants of capitalism) of the moment, so long as those ideologies stand to protect its interests.

The interests of capital have long been enmeshed with systems of oppression, division, and control that minimise class distinctions in favour of those of a commercially valuable national identity. Thus, our present capitalist conditions should be understood as conducive to any politics that maintains their dominant, or hegemonic status. The hyper-surveillance we experience through our engagement with smart technology is a factor in the (re)production of this hegemony.

Second, while the existence of early twentieth century fascism was in great part a resistance to a left-wing threat of which there is no comparable version in 'the West' today, fear of 'techno-fascism' carries an important point on the political tactics of the right, their political and economic purpose, and the ways in which these are applied through AI. As we discussed above, intensive data collection is a longstanding characteristic of colonialism and capitalism; it was also an important part of the Nazis' strategy to facilitate the Holocaust (Molnar 2024b, 121). And keeping with the US example, there is a substantial body of work on the 'emotive', divisive, and relatedly fascist character of Trump-era American politics (see Hall 2023, Berger 2025 and Merrin & Hoskins 2025). It is important that capitalism's proclivity for hyper-surveillance is understood as a causal rather than a preventative factor in the spectres of technofascism and authoritarianism.

Perhaps the most telling aspect of Boyle's provocation is his point on the indistinguishability of contemporary forms of control from their named and defined earlier manifestations. The way intense surveillance shapes every aspect of life in capitalist nations that profess liberty and ostensibly reject authoritarianism tells us a lot about where we are today. In the UK, for example, decades of neoliberalism have weakened trade unions, privatised public spaces, and restructured society based on being an individual consumer rather than part of a collective class interest that recognises it is in material opposition to the class interests of the rich (Gilbert & Williams 2022). Timcke (2021, 10) summarises:

> Conditions have never been more favourable for capitalism and more conducive to capital accumulation. Certainly, the digital revolution in telecommunications helps in that regard. But the naturalization of capitalist values is broader than just novel developments in technology. In addition to a labour regime shaped by the installation of neoliberal politics, intentional wage containment and a decline of union membership there is the ideological triumph of capitalism after the Cold War.

Wages have been suppressed, rents are soaring; it is difficult to conceptualise a meaning of life beyond individual survival and, hopefully, maybe, an accumulation of private profits that make surviving more comfortable. This basic narrative is woven into the fabric of our culture. Margaret Thatcher, who led the neoliberal restructuring of British society in the late twentieth century, famously said that 'economics are the method: the object is to change the soul' (Thatcher 1981). And as this neoliberal soul (one of intense individualism and dog-eat-dog principle) has consolidated its position, not only our proclivity but also our *capacity* for solidarity has diminished.

Theodoropoulos (2018, 318) explores the nature of class consciousness in the neoliberal workplace, where harsh working conditions and contract precarity define workers' experiences in the absence of trade unions that can defend their interests. Workplace organising feels out of reach, replaced by volatile and stressful conditions that 'leave little space for such thoughts' (Theodoropoulos 2018, 318). Companies hire people on temporary contracts and then mould them within a culture that demands they demonstrate their worthiness as an individual if they want to have any hope of being offered a secure and better-paid position. The only way 'out', is to buy in:

> Underneath the veneer of happiness and support, we are participants in an all-encompassing system of individualism and subtle but omnipresent competition that is designed to enter deep into our psyches. The more you participate, the more you reproduce it with a smile on your face ... these processes cultivate a vicious cycle of neoliberal individualism that makes collective dreams not only impossible, but unimaginable. (Theodoropoulos 2021)

In place of a class consciousness that empowers workers to imagine and win a future that gives them more control over their conditions, the 'neoliberal soul' renders the past and present something we must frantically escape from, as individuals, in the hope that we reach somewhere that affords us greater comfort and makes surviving a bit easier. In the frantic present, there is no time to form a coherent thought, a coherent memory of who we are in relation to structural power. Instead, all we see is the permanent contract, the promotion, the offer of greater security, and the bridges we must cross to get there—before anyone else does.

Hochuli (2024) refers to this sense of urgency as an outcome of 'hyper-politics: a sense of politics being everywhere and nowhere at the same time' as 'the modernist dream of speed has turned into a nightmare'. Where twentieth-century labour militancy was able to reclaim time from bosses in the form of reduced working hours, the nine-to-five now, in our period of neoliberal precarity, is for bosses 'an inconvenience, a regulatory artifice that only slows things down', and for workers, something to escape rather than fight:

> The traditional union tactic of 'working to rule' has been reborn as a desperate individualistic strategy: quiet quitting. Individuals are increasingly rejecting an unregulated, deinstitutionalized world that robs them of any sense of meaningful control. (Hochuli 2024)

This sense of time not only lost but also hard to grasp in the first place is a legacy of Thatcher's 'neoliberal soul'. We do not just lack the organisational capacity to slow this machine down; we have no time to figure out why either. This leads to what psychologists have called 'microefficiencies', small acts of productivity crammed into every second of the day. These behaviours, 'less about choice and more about survival ... driven by the belief that slowing down is unsafe or unproductive' (Hamilton 2025) are indicative of a burdened society, reduced to small acts of individual, micro resistance. With all of life permeated by this growing sense that things are out of control, going too fast, all we are left to do is cling on for dear life and try to make sense of the glimpses that might help us do so.

Big Tech is a political actor

Rendered organisationally, democratically, and somewhat intellectually impotent by the forces of capital, it is difficult for society to expose its contradictions and enact any control over their resolve. Memory, in these circumstances, is similarly beyond our control; it is increasingly shaped by technological conditions that we feed yet have no refrain over. As class consciousness has withered during the neoliberal period, so too has our capacity to resist the explanations of the tech elite.

In 2024, far-right groups rioted across the UK, and the anti-immigration Reform party recorded a significant vote share in the 2024 general election. The mainstream media and political class bear responsibility for sowing the seeds of unrest (Begum 2024). Since the beginning of the twenty-first century, the bipartisan consensus across Westminster and establishment media outlets has cultivated an accepted culture of Islamophobia. From a political perspective, this has helped to legitimise Britain's invasions of primarily Muslim countries (such as Iraq and Afghanistan), its support for the wars of strategic allies (such as Israel's genocidal colonisation of Palestine), and finally, so that the British public blames immigration for domestic social and economic crises instead of government policies. Increasingly alienated from control over the factors that shape their lives, such as housing, education, and healthcare, many people have found that the politics of the far-right at least give them a means of expressing their frustration, for these are a politics whose enemy is clear (if not materially accurate). As Abbas (2021, 404) puts it: 'the ontological insecurity that faces vulnerable groups whose loss of identity and the sense that they have no role in shaping their future existence leads them to become vulnerable to the Islamophobic forces that are generated by it'. This ontological insecurity is a result of social conditions that deprive communities of agency and, in the context of our digital media ecology, a fragmented memory that does not comprise coherent thought, experience, and understanding, but the popularised and commercialised shards of content, which gain personalised and algorithmic traction.

Despite having clear enemies (immigrants, but also LGBTQ+ people, women, and socialists), the politics of the far-right are full of contradictions. In the case of the summer 2024 riots in the UK, where much of the rhetoric targeted asylum seekers, one of these was: how can you win more power by attacking the powerless rather than the powerful?

You cannot, of course, which suits the powerful nicely. So why are these ideas and movements gaining so much traction in the West?

A full and comprehensive answer to this question is beyond the scope of this book. Yet in our analysis of capitalism's restructuring of memory, in part through a reorientation of class consciousness towards individualism, we can offer some explanation. The Big Tech industry is an active agent in politics as well as culture.

Technology and capitalism work cyclically in our society. They inform and drive each other. In 2024, Elon Musk, the man who topped Forbes' billionaire list, actively cheerleaded the far-right's actions in the UK from social media platform X (formerly Twitter), which he owns. His posts ranged from tweets suggesting the British police have a 'two tiered' system that cracks down harder on right-wing protestors than Muslim and pro-Palestine groups (Brown 2024), to retweeting fake news, such as a mock article claiming Prime Minister Keir Starmer had plans to open protestor 'detainment camps' in the Falklands for imprisoned rioters (Self 2024). Musk deleted that post after 35 minutes, by which time over 1.8 million people had seen it. He has previously taken to X to back anti-immigration and right-wing political figures such as then US presidential candidate Donald Trump (Musk 2024a) and Argentina president Javier Milei (Musk 2024b). Such a high-profile endorsement of the right from the owner and controller of an algorithmic platform (reported by Musk (Musk 2024c) to have 600 million monthly active users) shapes public opinion; clearly these are politicised spaces where certain ideas are given a lot of exposure. Indeed, Trump won the 2024 election, and Musk was awarded a role working with the US government. With social media fast becoming both a primary source of news, and the main setting where memories are not only made and stored but also given meaning (Jungselius & Weilenmann 2023), it is of grave concern that they are so beholden to the interests of the elites who control them.

Scottish economist George Kerevan (2024) identifies a distinction between the 'Big Six' Silicon Valley liberal globalists who have historically tended to back the US Democratic Party—Apple, Amazon, Alphabet (Google), Meta (Facebook), Microsoft, and Nvidia, and a new group of rogue tech oligarchs who more openly endorse a right-wing 'protectionism'—Elon Musk and Peter Thiel (of PayPal, data mining company Palantir, whose technology is used by the Israeli military in Gaza). While the former see the liberal status-quo as the most secure way to protect their assets (although, the aforementioned policy reversals by Meta indicate that loyalties are shifting), Musk, Thiel and others promote a politics which challenges this arrangement, to protect their own.

Donald Trump's running mate for the 2024 presidential election, JD Vance, was backed in the region of $15m by Thiel in his successful Ohio senate campaign. For Kerevan, Vance represents Big Tech's candidate for the presidency in 2028. The Project 2025 blueprint for Trump's presidency had been developed by right-wing Think Tank, the Heritage Foundation (of which Vance also has ties), and aims to deregulate banks and remove Joe Biden's AI regulations (which really aimed to protect the Big Six rather than the public anyway), so that US techno-capitalism can experience an unfettered expansion of wealth and power (Kerevan 2024). Evidently, the trajectory of AI and social media is inextricably tied to the trajectory of global capitalism. Paradoxically, like the memory it produces, it is highly ideological, yet opaque, 'open', and somewhat derived from a *total* archive, which makes these roots difficult to trace.

In this setting, Big Tech owners such as Musk can increase their sphere of influence, and society is left with two choices: the liberal-globalist techno-capitalists, or the far-right techno-capitalists. The former champion a status-quo politics that has presided over war, environmental collapse, and increasing global inequality over the last 40 years. The latter only stand to accelerate these problems. Neither is seemingly subject to meaningful democratic control.

Ours is a society where individuals and communities are increasingly alienated from the ability to express their agency, and as such, the story of what is happening in society is not just contested and repressed (by traditional propaganda) but fragmented, sharded, and distorted by algorithms that feed off emotion and outrage (engagement), and deny coherent thought. The chaos and precarity of neoliberal life strips away our ability to conceive of shared interests and futures we control, leaving us with little choice but to go it alone and jump through the next hoop, or climb the next rung, in the hope that this affords us something better. The past and present become something to escape, but never to understand. The interplay between how we remember, and how we are remembered, using technologies that disempower us in a society designed to reduce our collective empowerment, is cyclical, constantly reinforcing itself, established yet always evolving. This is the memory machine. We now turn to explore the new memory *process* through which the AI memory machine functions today.

3

The Memory Feed

Co-opted commodification

Technological development under capitalism has clear imperatives. The fragmentation and individualisation of memory is no accident. Our purchase and consumption of digitally driven services have explicit commercial and political interests. But what do these new conditions for memory mean for users and citizens? In this chapter, we explore this impact of the memory machine by analysing the routine but often invisible digital processes by which we are known through data and connectivity. Our data profiles, all our clicks, likes, and engagements, make a new memory of the self.

Consider how we give up and feed services and platforms, organisations and governments (or simply but massively, the internet) with our personal data and media content. The more we do this, the more we become digitally entangled, the more those who hold and use our data, messages, photos, videos, and so on, become more algorithmically enriched. In turn, the more that apps and platforms nudge and feed us versions and visions of that content, the more they can determine what is possible and impossible in memory in the future. The more we feed this machine, whose inner workings (algorithm) and embedded motivations (to generate financial and data capital) are not necessarily understood by us, chosen by us, owned by us, or even working in our interests, the more we empower it to form new and even humanly unknowable versions of the self and how we are remembered.

We call this process *the memory feed*, the principal means through which modern societies come to remember and forget.

This claim stems from the scale, complexity, and rapidity of the shifts in digital and AI-driven shaping of everyday and extraordinary memory.

The AI Memory Machine. Andrew Hoskins, Kristína Čimová, and Danny Pilkington,
Oxford University Press. © Andrew Hoskins, Kristína Čimová, and Danny Pilkington (2026).
DOI: 10.1093/oso/9780198995906.003.0003

It is now increasingly difficult to isolate memories that occur completely outside the realm of datafication, AI, and digital surveillance. In designers solving technical problems, how they shape a more frictionless user experience, new forms of accessing, sorting, storing, and using the past, once the imaginaries of fiction and fantasy, are increasingly made possible.

There is an app for everything, serving to ostensibly make life easier. Their focus is utility and convenience. We have apps to help us socialise in a world with less free social spaces (Cantor 2024) and apps to make the process of ordering a drink on an airplane more efficient and somehow better (Stewart 2023). But beyond these more mundane utilities, apps and platforms are providing ways of reckoning with life's most challenging tasks. For example, OttoStory (OttoStory 2025), an AI dictation tool that helps you write an autobiography, allows you to 'select a writing style that reflects your personality—whether adventurous, romantic or simply true to life'. Your personality, rather than being a subject of contestation among the people who know you, is something you define (read: *choose*, from a list of tone options), and then the AI *realises*. Already, the self here is something imagined, *un*remembered (Hoskins & Halstead 2021), co-created with the machine. Furthermore, your story is crafted through prompts that are 'designed by experienced psychologists to elicit meaningful and heartfelt responses, ensuring your story is rich with detail and emotion' (OttoStory 2025).

The human process of remembering a story and writing down, with all the effort, imperfection, and exclusion that comes with this, is cast aside. Now, for those who can afford access to the platform, your story is there to be told. But what are the implications for truth in stories that are elicited by algorithmic prompts? And what happens when a rival, cheaper AI model hits the market, offering a similar tool but for half the price, and with half of the data privacy rights? What becomes of these memories, never personally held, never to be personally owned?

Psychiatrist Alex Curmi (2024) considers whether such utility tools are worth the time they save us experiencing life on our own terms:

> Modern hyper-convenience is a kind of deal with the devil. It is seductive because it appeals to our instincts, but it surreptitiously depletes

> us. It has made it easier to get by, but in many ways harder to truly succeed. Human flourishing and happiness is not just about subsistence, but also depends on growth, dynamic problem-solving, and solidarity through hardship.

The risks in seeking to 'solve' hardship through AI have been put on stark display in Hans Block and Moritz Riesewieck's 2024 film, *Eternal You*, an exploration of the new and burgeoning market trend for devices and services that allow the living to 'speak' with AI driven avatars, which simulate human speech, facial expressions, and movements, of their deceased loved ones. The film highlights the emotionally warping experiences of users of this kind of commodification of immortality: 'There are things that scared me, and a lot of stuff I didn't want to hear—I wasn't prepared to hear'. Here companies can exploit both AI's capacity to help assuage human grieving, and the human and market-driven need for tools that do so. (We return to *Eternal You* and the wider concept of grief tech in Chapter 7). The proliferation of our unremembered selves impact not only the past left by the deceased, but also render the future open to new mass uncertainties of the extension and the recreation of a human-like memory changing and 'interacting' with others, beyond the lifespan of an individual.

In our introduction, above, we set out how we had spoken with industry experts. One of our app designer interviewees suggested that technological changes present challenges but also significant opportunities over time, in the ways in which our personal data can be made sense of and remade as memories. Their view was that data and individual memory are entwined in a cycle of inexorable production. The more data we give up, the more media content we record and share, the greater the array of ways in which we become remembered subjects, or objects. Thus, the utility and service of the memory feed improves (on its own terms at least) the more we find it useful or essential, the more we become embroiled.

Having enough data to give people with individuals' digital traces accumulating over years and decades, produces a different kind of feedback loop to the one imagined by the theorists of the extended mind (Clark 2008, Menary 2010). The individual is remembered by and through the accumulating personal data that we produce and knowingly or inadvertently share. And this loop is an ever-decreasing circle of autonomy, as algorithms, apps, platforms, designers, and owners become more efficient in targeting and nudging our memories, the more data they possess. As a result, people become 'co-opted into participating in their commodification' (Timcke 2021, 29). The memory of the self is something created in the feed, not quite wholly individual or collective, but something rather entangled in and emergent through the digital processes of you being known. In this way, Kroker writes of today's 'network ego':

> The network body has no memory other than its electronic traces, no sense of privacy that could possibly outpace its desire for connectivity, no perspective on augmentation that would not enable more complex looping of the cellular subject within relays of technological devices, software codes, satellite feeds, and always waiting mobile antennas. (2014, 106)

Memory in the feed then is not just a matter of emergence, namely the principal accident of the (re)formation of digital pasts, our perpetual haunting by an almighty dormant memory (Hoskins 2018, 382). Rather, today there is more of a radical emergence, in which memory of the self is not so much curated but rather *co-created*, with increasingly AI-driven technologies and services, promising to share and support our navigation through digital ecologies as a collaborative endeavour. The rapid growth of the AI 'companion', be this for relationships (Replika, Character.AI) or sex (Muah.AI, so-called uncensored AI), shows how rapidly the personal and private realms of life are being co-opted by and rendered reliant or dependent upon the machinic. To borrow from Microsoft's Copilot (Copilot 2025) (an AI companion for work), the past is also something already on Copilot today.

Memory in a lively human-centred sense is therefore fundamentally lost to the machine in the projection and immersion in companionship, in the technologies of the duplication, appropriation, algorithmic nudging, illumination, obscuration, and erasure of the human. These things called memories have a new tangible existence or non-existence, something to be processed, worked on, produced, organised, and archived, to enable their continued (re)production.

For instance, 'Memories' are part of Apple's operating system (Apple 2025); they have been appropriated through our subscriptions. The digital memory ecology is also a new memory economy. Apps and services are not merely retainers, stores, organisers, and curators of our memories, but rather something more relational, increasingly sold as a collaborative endeavour, giving the past new personal history and meaning.

Losing ourselves in a management of the past

Memories are certainly not about the past, but rather a presentist management of the self, identity, society. Digital memories are to be designed, they are ascribed an agency. This is not in terms of how remembering is usually thought of in that the already past can be shaped, suppressed, or enhanced in memory, or even in terms of a sense of a forthcoming significant event, like a wedding that is highly planned and choreographed for digital photography and video to secure the requisite record. Instead, there is a shift in focus to the creation and the *making* of memories. This is evident in popular culture and advertising where companies promote services that enable you to 'make memories', for events yet to be experienced.

This intensification of the apprehension for a future waiting to be recorded and turned into memory meets the compulsion to record everything, which in turn drives a feeling that the reality of experience requires some proof that life has been lived. Here we have the circularity of the memory feed (Figure 1). But this feeling of a highly personalised sense of the production and curation of your own memory feed is met with the fact that today's 'turning into memory' requires connection, distribution, and validation. As Merrin and Hoskins (2025, 43) argue, 'With the explosion of our own personalised realities and the connected foam of our bubble universes, we are all simultaneously conspiracists and co-respiracists'.

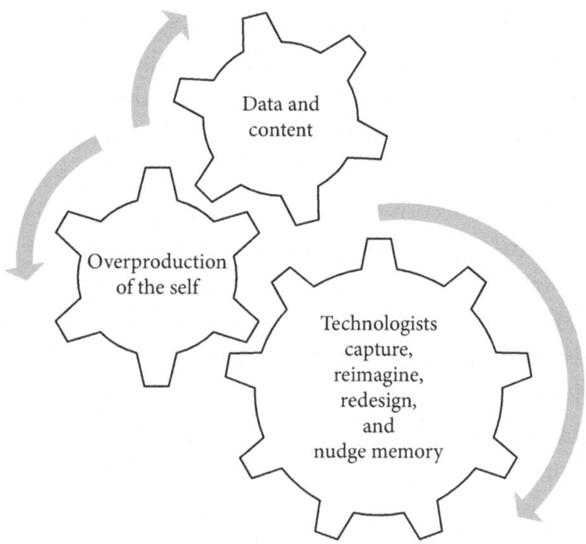

Figure 1 The memory feed

Life is thus a competition between us and everyone around us but also between us and our pasts, our former selves. The need to have a well-curated public (social media) and private (camera roll) documentation of life means present existence is measured against how good it will be to look back on, by us and by others. In this way, the past 'turns back on itself in order to anticipate how it will be regarded when it is completely past' (Hartog 2017, 114). Yet because we have not actually reached this future point, therefore, we cannot look back on what is happening just now; this vision is stuck in the present, experienced as a kind of closed circle (Hartog 2017, 114). Moreover, the more we are concerned about how a given photo, experience, or event will look as a past, the more technologies and apps help us render this vision a virtual and machine-collaborative reality, and the more we become dependent upon those same technologies and apps for memory in our memory feed.

The memory feed is how the more we feed our personal data and media content to apps and services, the more they become algorithmically attuned, and in turn, the more they nudge and feed us versions and visions of that content and determine what is possible and impossible in memory. As data, vibes, and trends swirl round about us, the self becomes oddly unremembered, in that it is untethered to a conceptualisation of ourselves based on anything deeper than that which we produce and are compelled to produce to attract warm applause from the emoji society.

Digital identities are co-produced by us and the algorithm guiding our engagement with digital spaces. This means our autonomy over these identities is limited. It is easy to see how this could lead to feelings of being lost, of being alienated from a sense of confidence over who we are. For instance, adolescents who spend more time on social media report lower levels of self-esteem than peers who use it less (Valkenburg et al. 2021, 70). Here is further circularity of the memory feed. The more we expose and promote our digital self, that which we do not fully recognise, the more we lose a grasp of ourselves.

Furthermore, although our algorithmic experiences are hyper-individualised and unique, they follow trends, and 'flatten culture' (Chayka 2024), we all end up consuming much of the same stuff. This means that over time, the further the unremembered self becomes embedded in the memory feed, the more personalised the world feels, in fact the more the algorithmically determined parts of us become increasingly aligned.

In the memory feed, there is a collusion of technology with the (digitally) remembered self, of convenience and control, of overload and sense-making. The tech gives us more, but then we need it more. Here there is a digital 'flywheel' (Collins n.d.) effect, whereby a relentless accumulation of and learning about the datafied individual leads to a tipping point. In our terms, this is the reaching of an unstoppable momentum of the production of digital memories.

It is not possible to identify the point at which the cycle of the production of the self, the accumulation of data and the reflexive design for digital living, broke through to being irreversible under present technological conditions, but it is a character feature of the digital flywheel effect that we did not notice it. One of our designer interviewees suggested that 2011 was the tipping point from a reliance to dependency on digital tech and services, for everyday life, communication, work, relationships, education, and so on.

In the field of media and memory studies, there is an interesting trend in publications around this time, all pointing to a more restless, feed-like, or at least mobile, conceptualisation of memory of the day. For instance, 'memobilia' (Reading 2009), 'multidirectional' (Rothberg 2009), 'connective' (Hoskins 2011), 'travelling' (Erll 2011), 'mobile' (Hirsch 2014), and 'on-the-fly' (Hoskins 2014). And the machinic past was also more explicitly characterised in Sluis' (2010) 'algorithmic memory'. As Sluis wrote then: 'When the collection and distribution of media becomes the collection and distribution of data, our digital memories become subject to the economics of information production and knowledge management' (Sluis 2010).

Yet today's memory feed is not only how the past becomes that which is fed to us—algorithmically tailored and prescribed in apps and services—but also that which we feed it—for our friends, family, and subscribed publics. In other words, it is the overproduction of the self that enables the paradoxical mix of the personal and the algorithmic curation of the past.

Some digital content we may explicitly recognise and treat as a kind of 'memory', as with memory apps such as *1 Second Everyday* and *Apple Memories*. Yet, everyone, as well as overproducing the present, is also churning up past content that is now layered and speculated on in new ways in that same present.

Consider the example of the 2022 Russian invasion of Ukraine. The digital feed of this war is an astonishing fractalising of messages, images, memes, videos, live feeds, TikToks, Telegram channels, tweets, and satellite mapping, as well as a frenzy of mainstream media news through which the past was inserted and reframed anew. The past has long been inserted into commentary and framing of emergent events, for instance, through its constant referencing and re-referencing in a journalistic déjà vu. However, the Russia–Ukraine war is unique in the speed and scale of the deployment of instantly available web and social media archives of images, videos, and memes, in a constant competition to shape interpretations of events unfolding on the ground in Ukraine.

Yet at the same time that past wars are being churned up and used as a prism of emergent warfare, there is also a new radical accumulation of images and videos from the intense overproduction of this war in the digital feed—a *radical* war (Ford & Hoskins 2022). Just consider, for example, the number of smartphones, drones and other connected devices in the battlefield that Ukraine has become. The individualised production of this event, enabled by the smartphones of those experiencing, fighting, and subject to this war, has produced the most personalised and the most documented event in history.

But what of the memory feeds of this war will survive or remain accessible or searchable, and to whom in 10, 20, or 30 years? What apps, services, platforms, and internet structure will remain? What will be the purpose of this evidence and how will we measure its veracity? Who gets to decide? The (social) media overproduction of this war at the level of the individual and the related mass uploading and sharing of images or video (for instance, of alleged war crimes (Bassu 2022)) offer the prospects of a fantastic archive of war. Yet, will splintering, fragmentation, loss and erasure, and ultimately inaccessibility and relatedly forgetting, be the more likely outcome? How can a story be linear (yet still contestable) when it is told through a Big Tech-owned lens of fragments?

It is difficult to argue against a version of history if the version is constantly shifting, subject to deletion, re-ordering, and revision, swirling in data patterns that are beyond human comprehension. All wars and their meanings have been re-imagined, contested and legitimised, remembered and forgotten, through shifting technologies and media of capture and representation. War accelerates into media, as media accelerates into war. Yet the digital and AI eras render these processes of representation and mediation precarious, a new age of uncertainty of the past, in their slippage from human comprehension as well as control.

The very process of the overproduction of the self transforms the memory of the self. But for all the active participation in the production of their self, what becomes of memories is increasingly determined by the agents, technologies, and processes of societies that are awash with data. And we are tied into a much larger digital flywheel or flywheels of memory, which are together splintering shards of the memories of all of us, into uncertain futures.

There is no authentic You

The development of the memory feed shapes a broader trend of a much greater individuation of the ways in which the past is dealt with and discussed. Today, the digital self is the central producer of the past. Whereas the mass media used to produce content for us, the audience, to consume, technologists now create platforms and apps so that we can produce ourselves.

Here we return to Frankie Boyle's (2022) interrogation of Western culture and society in the age of AI. The novel's protagonist, Felix explores whether taking acid could actually help to provide some clarity in the maelstrom of entwined production and consumption. He compares 1960s counterculture with its equivalent, or lack of, now:

> I think that people in the sixties would be frightened by how little counterculture there is now, how uncontested our shared illusions are .... Before, there was propaganda, but now you go online and exist within the propaganda. You're moderated by the trips of thousands of other people. Now there's no authentic trip to be had, and maybe no you to have it. (Boyle 2022, 126–127)

Whatever you think of 1960s counterculture, whether it was subversive or indeed contrived and superficial itself, the point the character Felix is making holds some truth. Ideological propaganda once worked on a loop: produced by the media, then received and negotiated by an audience, whose reaction would then form the public opinion targeted during the next propaganda production (Hall 1980). Ideas were propagated and resisted with more coherence and relation to class interest, as their origins could be more easily traced and their embedded interests identified in a more straightforward fashion. In the context of British propaganda, people consumed news as narratives coming from few official sources or mainstream providers. Cultural reactions to these therefore had a discernible basis, a traceability, and, crucially, an authenticity of some kind. While the propaganda was the same, individuals and communities' negotiation of it differed greatly. These were conditions for originality. Society consumed media, accepting, negotiating, or opposing its intended message (Hall 1980), before spitting back out an analysis or a perception that could reflect people's experiences and class interests.

By contrast, now, everyone experiences their own propaganda. And because of the memory feed, our reactions to it become more similar over time: 'there's no authentic trip' (read: experience) as everyone else's individual experiences and motivations touch, or *influence*, the social media space and the valuation—both socially and financially—of the self within it. Volpe (2024), for example, observes that in the age of social media, 'authenticity is increasingly communicated through a personal brand, which is necessary in order to gain a following and further career aspirations'.

Thus, in certain media, corporate, cultural, and academic professions at least, it is increasingly difficult if not impossible to excavate the real you from the you that you have identified as saleable, mapped out within the context of social media and its expectations, and then overproduced. For Jennings (2024), this can have particularly negative consequences for many artists, who rather than allowing themselves to be truly authentic, instead find themselves engaged in 'constant self-promotion in the form of cheap trend-following, ever-changing posting strategies, and the nagging feeling that what you are really doing with your time is marketing, not art'. How bleak, that in cultivating our legacies in the age of social media, our attention must be so cunningly split, with one eye on finding a true kernel of original self, and the other eye on finding a trend to sell it with. It is worth noting that even in professions where the social media marketing of the self is less relevant, if relevant at all, neoliberalism's introduction of competitive individualistic ideals across workplaces means there is likely at least some incentive for a degree of self-marketisation.

The process creates a homogeneity of hyper-individualised experiences. Your online algorithm is yours, in that it is specifically reflective of your interactions, yet you do not own or control it, and despite its specificity to you, it compels you towards trends born out of commercial interest rather than resistance to it. Notwithstanding the fact that physical neoliberal society is designed to limit our space and capacity to resist it through culture, within its virtual context, our selves are moderated by an opaque algorithm that both games and is gamed by everyone, all in the name of its primary objective: commercial interest. The risk therefore is that eventually this imperative, broadly understood as self-marketisation and commercial interest, will be so deeply woven into our algorithmically produced selves, that 'all existing [capitalist] social relations may be encoded, meaning that social inequality will be programmed into social infrastructure'. (Timcke 2021, 154)

A perilous newfound convenience

> Convenience is often trivially associated with a progressive better, clearer and faster functioning for all of us. (Szakolczai 2023, 11–12)

Overproduction and individualisation are the entwined drivers of the memory feed. For all the feeling of individual will and control that the obsessive digital capturing of the present affords, we need to ask, what does this accumulation result in? What kind of reality will then be findable, usable again, as any kind of meaningful memory? There is after all no such thing as a benign archive. Memory, its future presence, absence, and accessibility, are being held hostage by the machine.

One of the key smartphone transformations of memory is that its portability and convenience of use enable an ongoing capacity to record and document the everyday, the mundane as well as the exceptional. This newfound convenience is on such a level that it is difficult to imagine life before or without it. One of the memory app CEOs we spoke with, in experimenting with a prototype, had this revelation: 'it was only after a couple of weeks of doing it that I was like, "Oh wow, this is working. This is easy. I doubt I'm not going to have an iPhone in my pocket anytime soon ever again"'.[1]

Thus, it is the everyday and its potential to be continuously monitored and captured and shared through the individualised tech of the smartphone that makes the future past newly and continuously vulnerable to being reordered, remade, and retained, as well as overburdened, overconsumed, and obliterated.

The revolution in digital memory is partly in the radical uncertainty of what kind of past of this era will ever be findable, accessible, and usable. The current culture of sharing on social media and the desire for exposure and contagion of one's messages, images, self, collapses the traditional distinctions of memory as being personal and public, individual and social, ephemeral and enduring. Although social media and some memory apps facilitate and encourage the sharing of everything, some enable a more nuanced management of memories deemed not for public exposure, be they considered as mundane, personal, or distressing. *1 Second Everyday* is one such app, as Cesar Kuriyama, designer and CEO, explained:

> We get so many emails; we get so many messages. There are a lot of people that record the bad stuff. That shoots off into a lot of people who share it and they want to share it to show a balance, not just highlights Reel Instagram style. One of the things that we hear over and over again, from our customers is, 'I use 1 Second Every Day to fill in the gaps on the things I wouldn't post on Facebook or Instagram'. It's like, Instagram, Facebook, right? 'Check out me, I'm skiing', or whatever. There's a lot of parts of our lives that are really important, meaningful to us as individuals that we don't think is that interesting to people outside of ourselves.
>
> Each month, *1 Second Everyday* provides a collaged summary video. It's a 30-second long: 'Here's my June 2021', and users frequently post these publicly when they are released. Mundane moments interspliced throughout life actually plays out pretty well as a strategy. The users probably wouldn't post it as an individual moment, but intermixed into their month, they feel like it creates a balance of: 'Look, my life is not about skiing every day. My life is me just at home, working. Then I'm with the kids and then I'm with my parents and then I'm experiencing another cool concert or whatever'. It's a wide spectrum of information harnessed to counter what a lot of people don't tend to share, because it's too personal.[2]

The app shows that people are keen to capture mundane moments as well as profound ones, deeming them worth keeping as part of their memory record, as part of the continuity and completeness of their life experience. Moreover, *1 Second Everyday* offers users a way to manage traumatic memories precisely through their incorporation into a context of a month or more of memory. Such difficult memories are folded into the video along with every other day, perhaps diminishing their uniqueness and reducing their presence to a matter of one-second excerpts; users cannot dwell on them in the way they could with a still image or photograph.

It is easy to see why life is becoming increasingly livestreamed: the tools are there for it, and once you accept that they are *the* place to store and share memories, the scope of their value only increases with greater use. For the best returns on your data investment, invest more data. For a complete memory, send a complete dataset.

The *1 Second Everyday* app provides a short video representation of memory, and this represents something of a departure in meaning from photographs as stand-alone representations. In our current era of excess imagery (including of oneself), one view is that the single image stands out, rescuing memory from the incessant visual flow in which it is so easy to become lost. Susan Sontag wrote influentially about the effects of this distinction:

> Nonstop imagery (television, streaming video, movies) is our surround, but when it comes to remembering, the photograph has the deeper bite. Memory freeze-frames; its basic unit is the single image. In an era of information overload, the photograph provides a quick way of apprehending something and a compact form for memorizing it. The photograph is like a quotation, or a maxim or proverb. (2003, 22)

Yet today, the photograph, the restful and contemplative still image, seems ever more elusive. And although there are exceptions, for instance an occasional news image that may momentarily stand out, that does arrest the flow, these seem harder to find today than in earlier media ecologies, not so awash with moving content. Instead, nonstop imagery, in Sontag's terms, has a whole new existence, as a primary mode of communication. The short video is a dominant form of digital communication for the brand new, born-digital generation, who we are calling Generation F—for Forget. Instant messaging apps such as Snapchat and TikTok have revolutionised the visual world of the relatively young (with the rapid increase in smartphone ownership by teens and pre-teens).

TikTok enables users to create short-form videos with music, filters, and other features, which can be easily and instantly shared, including via other social media platforms and networks. It is the ultimate facilitator of the pervasive 'self-paparazzization' (Merrin & Hoskins 2025) of the everyday, in other words the constant digital streaming of life. In these circumstances, if we accept Sontag's vision (above) of the photograph as having the 'deeper bite' in memory, then the memorial prospects of Generation F seem shallow. This view is not an attempt to blame a new generation for the effects of social media use, but rather to recognise the astonishing speed and scale of the transformation in everyday communication and sociability and to attempt to consider how this effects memory. To this end, we now develop the idea of 'Generation F' and the experience of remembering and forgetting in the memory feed.

4

Generation F for Forgetting

Generational differences

Our analysis of the memory feed, and indeed the wider concept of the memory machine, is a provocation on the ways in which the conditions for memory in the age of AI have transformed into something fundamentally new, despite having roots in a long dominant capitalist system. Much of our discussion so far has outlined how capitalist technological development has traceable characteristics across time and technologies, yet in the age of AI, it is producing a set of conditions that, in the context of memory, are quite novel. Namely, these are a shift away from human and contestable processes of memory-making, towards a dependency on algorithmic technologies that provide personalised views through the same narrow lens, with memory left as something, in great part, generated by and for the machine. Crucial to exploring the nature and magnitude of this change then requires reflection on how we were once remembered and forgotten.

For older generations, this capacity is there. But what if all we had ever known had come through the memory feed? What if everything we remember and forget is conditioned by these circumstances, leaving us unable to conceive of the making of memory somehow outside of them?

With the growing influence of the memory feed, this is a reality creeping in for the online generations, primarily Generation Z ('Zoomers') born between 1997 and 2012) and Generation Alpha (those born from the early 2010s to mid-2020s) (Höfrová, Balidemaj & Small 2024). Across these younger Gen Z and Gen A cohorts, spans a group whose conditions for memory can be defined through its relationship with fast-emerging digital technologies and media. We call this group **Generation F(orget).**

The AI Memory Machine. Andrew Hoskins, Kristína Čimová, and Danny Pilkington,
Oxford University Press.
DOI: 10.1093/oso/9780198995906.003.0004

Generation F spans the two tipping points we identified in Chapter 1, above, namely an early 2010s shift from human reliance, to a dependency, on digital mechanisms and services for the making and the losing of memory, to the 2020's emergent, addictive AI-generated services and agents, such as AI companions.

And like multiple digital flywheel effects, wherein a relentless accumulation of and learning about the datafied individual by the tech and technologists creates an unstoppable momentum of the memory feed, it seems that this generation, on society's current trajectory, might have passed a point of no return.

The memory produced through the memory feed, and its reflection of a fragmented society defined by capitalism embedded, unrecognised, and unaccountable, is likely to be the only memory left. There is no real social experience unmediated by its record in the virtual realm, thus there is no memory unobscured by the capitalist lens through which we produce it, share it, engage with it, and remember it. As Hochuli (2024) summarises in his discussion of transformations in time,

> Societies generally undergo radical transformation around once in a generation, but at some point in the past decades, that rate has accelerated, so that change is now *intra*generational. This erodes the conditions for coherence and continuity in one's personal identity.

This is a world in which the algorithmically overproduced individual is the primary self. And to reiterate, a key feature of the tipping point from reliance to dependency of human memory on digital apps and platforms, is that it was not noticed. What defines the era of Generation F then is their riding the wave of video-messaging apps (see the section in Chapter 6 on memory through multisensory (virtual) experience). Their use is not some kind of extension of what we once called the 'consumption' of media, or any development of that listening or watching group once known as an 'audience'. Instead, these are images and videos employed as a primary and immediate means of communication between individuals, and their subscribed publics. Not only is there a dependency on tech for memory, but rather tech provides the fundamental site where memories are made, stored, and given meaning.

Generation F is messaging, snapping, and TikTok-ing their experience of the present into existence and possibly into oblivion. The memory feed is then a paradoxical creation—the more the individual and the individual's experience becomes mediatised, rendered as a form of media, the more it becomes humanly uncertain, out-of-control of the hands of the very user that snapped or shared it. Surely then, it is Gen F that are generating the most precarious of memories.

New media for a new generation

Defining work in assessing the relationship between the media of the day and the generational memory of that day is found in Ingrid Volkmer's (2006) 'Global Generations Media' project. This research sampled the formative years of three generational groups and the associated media of the time ('print/radio', 'black-and-white television', and 'Internet'). Drawing upon the sociologist Mannheim's (1952) idea of generational 'entelechies', it sought to see if the structuring of the common experiences of each generation, could be related to its experience of media. Thus, as Volkmer (2006, 7) argues, this framework was aimed at showing 'the relevance of the media environment for generation-specific perceptions of the world, despite national, cultural, and societal differences'. One of the researchers on the project found that, whereas in the older cohorts of the Global Generations Media work, 'media memories were specific to a technology ... younger generations were awash in media product. As media become more enveloping, the source became less important' (Slade 2006, 207). Think of how the wider concept of 'the algorithm' is beginning to transcend the importance of the platform it exists in. No longer do we tell our friends, 'I keep getting ads on Facebook' for x, y, or z product; now we increasingly say, 'my algorithm keeps showing me' x, y, or z product.

It is clear to us that the distinctions between generations and the time passing between them was previously true to the etymology of a generation, i.e., members of the 'baby boomer' generation could comfortably be the parents of the next generation to come. However, this generational gap has shrunk. Today, Generation F, born digital, overlapping with Generation Z and A, and not far enough from the Millennial Generation Y to be their offspring either. For instance, Gumpert and Cathcart (and somewhat ahead of the field in writing in the mid-1980s) suggest that:

> Prior to the late nineteenth century media explosion, generations came and went, all exposed to and acquiring the same print grammar. Thus media seemed to have little bearing on human time relationships. Though we still think of people as related, or separated in chronological generation time, the rapid advent of new media and the acquisition of new media grammars implies new alignments, shorter and more diverse than those based on generations. (Gumpert & Cathcart 1985, 31, cited in Bolin 2016, 11)

However, the smartphone disrupts the continuity of change in the relationship between the media and the generation of the day. As a personally attached mobile device, the smartphone (and by extension, the smartwatch) shapes a new digital memory ecology of the individual. This is not only an immediate and potentially constant means of recording the everyday (photography, video, audio) but also of its potentially immediate and constant means of sharing of the everyday and everything via an array of apps and social media and so on, including in real time.

The smartphone is not a medium in the traditional sense of the term. Rather, it is a portal, a hub for hyperconnectivity with others, with the world, as well as a computer. It is a single device that effectively enables the many features long said to be important to remembering and/or forgetting—recording, storing, archiving, witnessing, sharing, remediating, and deleting. The smartphone is a change in kind compared with the media associated with the consumption of earlier generations (also all available on a smartphone), notably through its facilitating of participation.

Other functions of media are subsumed by the smartphone in its capacity to apprehend other media and communicational forms, including AI-driven services, which place the individual at the centre of their own ecology. Even the very first smartphones had more computational power and capabilities than the Apollo 11 space shuttle, which landed man on the Moon. The smartphones of today have abilities that the Generation X or even Y could not have fathomed would be possible to carry around in one's pocket.

The break with the temporal tradition had started already by the shortening of this span by the Millennials, whose social media and general digital activity has been well documented. For example, we know that the Millennials are much more likely to have several different profiles on different websites (Nielsen and Company 2015), are more prone to internet addiction and impulse-control disorders (Christakis et al. 2011), are also more prone to social media addiction (Kuss and Griffiths 2011, Andreassen et al. 2012), and more vulnerable to the ready availability of the stimulus and the social comparisons with peers when it comes to the digital ('all my friends are on it') (Martin et al. 2013).

However, for Generation F, there is another step change in immersion in connected technologies. Kleiser and Bright argued in 2019 that the ubiquity and perceived value of social media has made it one of the 'everyday things', such as food or exercise, that we are much more likely to be addicted to than anything that takes place out of the ordinary (cited in Grover et al. 2011). Excessive social media use begets an inevitable detachment from the responsibilities of real life, reorienting users towards virtually constructed relationships. (Balcı & Karaman 2020, 1216). This is a marked shifting of the paradigm from social media being an accessory to everyday life, to social media becoming everyday life. True to Carr's (2020) observation, therefore, Generation F lives in a 'world of interruptions' much more than any other generation before, by nature of constantly interrupting their day-to-day lives with a compulsive use of the digital (Carr 2020). This inevitably leads to a fetishisation of the mundane and its turning into a spectacle. The act of recording has in fact become more urgent than experiencing that which is recorded (Hoskins & Halstead 2021).

It follows, therefore, that if Millennials were found to prioritise social media above other activities (Cabral 2011) and were found to need social media to achieve satisfaction, then Generation F will have this concept as a starting point, a building block on which a whole lifestyle dependent on connectivity, sharing, oversharing, streaming, and obsessive recording rests, and upon which it also crumbles. This level of compulsion to record and use the smartphone as the new locus of the self is reinforced through the social circles and networks accessed by Generation F online. The importance of acceptance within these digital networks (defined as family, friends, colleagues, peers, and others who socialise online) cannot be overstated and turns this overuse of the digital into another marker of Gen F. This is the generation that utilises social networking and media out of habit and convenience more than any before, mostly because they have never experienced another way of accessing information and have never experienced a different avenue of personal validation in a social group.

In an interview with journalist Alfie Packham, 30-year-old Maanuv Thiara laments the generational transition from library use to search engine use: 'Yeah, the internet's free and we've all got smartphones. But I feel like when I'm Googling stuff, I'm inherently distracted. I've got 17 tabs open at the same time. In the library, you can focus' (Packham 2024). Thiara, a Millennial, is able to identify the distinction between former ways of learning and encoding memories and the new methods afforded by the internet. In this sense, we see the Millennial Generation Y as a bridging generation between those born digital and those born without the digital, and we see Generation F as a generation within which the use of the digital is not just instilled, but is a necessary feature of the processing of information and memory. In this way, they become subjects of what Couldry and Hepp (2016) call 'deep mediatization'—a process of embedding the media in social processes in a much more intense way than ever before.

Deep mediatisation

This intense embedding of the media in social processes leads to the implosion of formerly distinct mechanisms and agents, so, as Roisin Kiberd puts it in *The Disconnect*, it has become 'difficult to separate human from machine, mediation from emotion, selfishness from love' (Kiberd 2021). The past is caught up and produced through these same entanglements and demands, with memories from a particular holiday, month, season, or even a whole year reliant or dependent upon a 15-second algorithmically generated *Memories* video, displayed for the smartphone.

It is no wonder then that the restless and mobile conceptualisations of media and memory we observed in Chapter 3, are complemented by ideas in the human sciences as to the use of technology in 'cognitive offloading' (see Chapter 6). This includes how 'transactive memory systems' involve the sharing of memories not only amongst people but between people and objects and devices, including the smartphone (Soares and Storm 2018). With the connective turn and deep mediatisation, important work has recognised the increasing complexities and effects of cognitive offloading for the persistence and the functioning of memory (Barnier 2010; Risko 2019);Wang 2022; Risko et al. 2024).

Some, like Kiberd, see the spread of digital living as responsible for contemporary individual maladies, including individuals seduced to fall into the countless rabbit holes of information on the internet, developing sleep and eating disorders through the constant potential for distraction, and digital and AI forms of intimacy displacing human face-to-face encounters. She offers a fierce account of the digital's fostering of self-destructive tendencies, with the human mind of this century vulnerable to an array of instantly available digital and AI-driven solutions offered to meet a myriad of communication, logistical, and relationship challenges.

However, our analysis here goes beyond accounting for the impairing effects of the internet on memory (Sparrow, Liu & Wegner 2011, Yamashiro and Roediger 2019) or personalised accounts of addictive, detrimental behaviour, induced by an abandonment of contact in that once called In Real Life (IRL). Key for us are the structural conditions for this impairment, the social base at the root of their (re)production, which leaves individuals continually and increasingly unable to enact any control over their resolve. Crary (2013, 37), for example, summarises that 'our perceptual and cognitive relationship to communication and information technology will continue to be estranged and disempowered because of the velocity at which new products emerge and at which arbitrary reconfigurations of entire systems take place'. In other words, we are always one step behind the technology that redefines what we consider to be personal or lasting.

To capture these structural conditions of the AI memory machine then, instead of cognitive offloading, a more adept description of the processes here would be cognitive *extraction*, to highlight the uses and abuses of the memory of you in the wild. A useful distinction here is between personal and 'really personal' data. Really personal data is information about us that reveals more than just personal data, so it can be used in more ways against us. This is data that both expresses and exposes us, including details of our opinions, emotions, relationships, sexuality and its expression, and our bodies and health. This sort of data was not previously possible to harvest at the magnitude of today through ever-expanding and ever-smarter, relentlessly learning algorithmic processes.

The collection of data today goes further than in previous eras, combining to shape a more holistic view of you, with the linking up of every captured behavioural action, every micro-second of physical location, typing, action, thought, expression, interaction, message, aspiring to a totality. William Merrin's (2014, 92) work is prescient here in his discussion of a new internal relationship, 'in which it is not God but one's ISP, one's search engine, web mail provider, social networking site, favourite bookstore or pornography-site-of-choice, that now knows that intimate interior 'you''.

The deep mediatisation process maps onto this idea of a self that is rendered minable and knowable in more granular, intimate and holistic ways, including beyond human forms of intelligibility and autobiography.

When we talk about the external social conditions of memory 'in the wild', with regards to media, we mean the individual and group experiences and practices of creating, recoding, archiving, uploading, liking, clicking, and sharing messages, images, videos, and so on, that might enhance or diminish human memory for a moment or event. Considering the relationship between media and the conditions of external memory is important. But a new digital memory *ecology* approach goes further. A key shaper of memory in the wild is through its 'mediatization'. This is the process by which everyday life is increasingly embedded in and penetrated by **connectivity**: the process of shifting interconnected individual, social and cultural dependency on media, for maintenance, survival, and growth (Hoskins 2014). The process of mediatisation is not even, and memory ecologies are not uniform. Deep mediatisation can therefore be characterised as a 'wave of digitalization and datafication' that leads to 'much more intense embedding of media in social processes than ever before' (Couldry & Hepp 2016). The processes of digitalisation drive a rise of the individual as centre of their own media worlds, a collapse in trust in mainstream media and politics, and a loss of faith, certainty, and security in history (Happer, Hoskins & Merrin 2019). Datafication is the continuous generation of data about people, their acts and events, so that a new form of power is exercisable by 'those with access to databases, processing power, and data-mining expertise' (Andrejevic 2014, 1676, Livingstone 2019, 171). And as we highlighted in Chapter 2, this is a power dynamic that has been captured and applied in favour of the interests of capital, at the expense of the agency of those being datafied (Timcke 2021, 3–4). Such an ecology deprives us of control.

Deep mediatisation then, takes the really personal data we may have imparted unconsciously, through exploratory clicks, hesitant scrolls, and lingering pauses over content, and then uses this data more invasively. In this way, the data world of today has become the key battleground for privacy, identity, and memory.

The normalisation of public exposure

In our framework, therefore, Generation F is the generation that is most likely to be subject to deep mediatisation and its extractive forces, and is also most likely to have the least amount of control over its data. It is the generation subject to a paradox in being most likely to be known comprehensively through data, yet least likely to have a humanly conceived perception of itself. For instance, for Gen F 'oversharing' is a kind of new normal, what it is to live in and with a digital ecology. This trend is evident in the failure of attempts to temper the accessibility and reach of digital memory about you. For instance, the European 2012 legislation on the Right to Be Forgotten (RtbF) which was once considered to be a breakthrough in the preservation of personal information online, is no longer sufficient, if it ever was (Hoskins 2014). Later enshrined in Article 17 of the EU General Data Protection Regulation, the RtbF gives a person the right to have their personal data deleted in certain circumstances (GDPR.EU 2026) For us, the RtbF is symptomatic of a sense of a loss of control over the memory feed.

Instead, the right not to be known should be an urgent pursuit.[1] This is demonstrated in several recorded events of public rejection of the invasive nature of data usage. For example, in 2019, the online platform endgadget.com reported a story of a teenager suing Apple for $1bn, claiming that facial recognition in a string of Apple robberies led to their false arrest (Moon 2019). In 2017, Global News reported that a Canadian vibrator manufacturer agreed to pay compensation for tracking owners' use, which revealed intimate information such as temperature and vibration intensity about the customers (Bogart 2017). Clearly, the intimate and really personal domains are no longer considered private and secure, and their capturing through rapidly evolving technological processes poses a threat to our own self-knowledge as much as our capacity to recognise ourselves.

Nicholas Carr articulates this shift of self-recognition in his book *The Shallows* (first published in 2010) invoking Descartes and his belief (which has since been proven valid by the study of neuroplasticity) that our thought processes can exert a physical influence on the physiological: 'we become, neurologically, what we think' (Carr 2020, 33). According to Carr (2020,44), the 'tools of the mind' in the twenty-first century are most prominently the intellectual technologies that we use to extend our mental powers; anything from a newspaper or a globe to the internet, and the smartphone.

Carr (2020, 45) argues that these tools 'have the greatest and most lasting power over what and how we think. They are our most intimate tools, the ones we use for self-expression, for shaping personal and public identity, and for cultivating relations with others'. It then follows that these tools will have a huge impact on the mechanisms of our thinking, but they also shape how and what we can remember and forget. We propose that a split with linear thinking, long encouraged by tools such as physical books, which force the reader to apply prolonged focus and attention to the content, by the primary tool of distraction—the smartphone—turning text into countless hyperlink-able rabbit holes, is the stuff of normality for the Generation F. This is a generation growing up decades into neoliberalism that, as we have discussed in Chapter 2, has changed the soul of society into something grotesquely individualistic, with a diminished capacity for collective critical thought. Between longer working hours for less money, shut down libraries and community centres, and smartphone addiction, who has the time to think things through anymore? Who has the time to form memories? Why would you, when your phone has everything on it anyway?

The tensions of the neoliberal soul play out across society, including the arts and literature. In Kevin Bridges' (2023, 293–294) novel, *The Black Dog*, young philosopher, Doof Doof observes that for Generation F, the digital ecology is restructuring consciousness in such a way that puts a squeeze on human emotion and reflection:

> All we have is distractions, now, it's a huge market, maybe we've ended up *too* immersed in the trivial and not left any time for sadness .... Like, we were never designed to be as happy as the modern world, the internet – Facebook and all that – is trying to make us. I think anyway. Maybe we'll evolve over time, to catch up, but just now we're the first ones to take the hit (Bridges 2023, 293–294)

As such, it reasonably follows that the thinking and memory-making processes of Generation F are removed from those of the Generation Y's and X's. The memories of Generation F therefore risk turning into, and perhaps irrecoverably have turned into, something that older generations cannot relate to anymore. The memory of Generation F to some extent must, logically, be equally as torn, distracted, non-linear, and fragmented as the thinking process from which it was conceived, through a series of hyper-linked rabbit holes, threads, half-read articles, and pinging notifications about this, that, the next thing, *everything*. This is a memory that, in the traditional sense experienced by previous generations, is over.

The normalisation of algorithmic decision-making

Of course, for such a drastic transformation to be achieved, Generation F would need to be at least somewhat sold on the benefits of this post-human future. The concept of 'hegemony' helps to illuminate this problem. Drawing on the work of early twentieth-century Italian philosopher, Antonio Gramsci, hegemony, broadly speaking, refers to 'the ideological domination of one social group over others: the exercise of a degree of "intellectual and moral leadership" over subordinates that diminishes the need for direct, coercive measures to ensure compliance' (Martin 1997, 38). In other words, hegemony is achieved when society consents, either actively (with buy-in) or passively (with resigned acceptance) (Gilbert & Williams 2022), to the ruling group's vision of how things should work.

For Generation F, the vision they are confronted with supposes that AI can, will, and should become a guiding constituent in everyday life. AI technologists propose that now, in many ways, 'AI is raising Gen Alpha as much as parents and teachers are' (Code Entropy 2024), and Gen Z is seen as 'true pioneers in this AI-driven era' (Erkul 2023). Young people are being thrust to the forefront of AI's implementation and are, as a result, its willing or unwilling guinea pigs (see Chapter 6).

Research shows that while children and adolescents decreasingly use the internet for research and creative activities, they demonstrate an awareness that algorithms invade their privacy and become 'creepy' (Vallejos et al. 2021, 4–14). Having grown up with social media and increasingly AI technologies, Generation F are tech savvy and aware that algorithms hold a great deal of knowledge about us and therefore power. Similarly, many young people know how to work algorithms to their advantage, through certain likes, clicks, and online behaviours (De Groot, de Haan & van Dijken 2023), and studies find that despite their generational position, high-school students are capable of engaging with and leading philosophical discussion on the pros and cons of generative AI for education and indeed humanity more broadly (Higgs & Stornaiuolo 2024, 639–641). Indeed, recent research reveals that young people are challenging the inevitability of growing up online, putting self-imposed limitations on their screen time and content consumption

(Hall 2025). It is evident that for many of Gen F, there remains a capacity for critical engagement with what AI is. Far from being passive users and consumers, children, adolescents, and young people are acutely aware of the dangers of social media, and their gaming and managing of the platforms should be understood as evidence of their capacity to offer resistance (see Chapter 8).

However, it is not clear how this awareness is translatable into enhanced agency in an age where the influence of AI—unmanaged, unmitigated, or unmediated by human choice—is growing fast. De Groot, de Haan, and van Dijken (2023, 710–711) summarise:

> One could speculate that the environments the younger generations grow up in are often offering automatically-selected content based on algorithmic filtering without users specifically asking for content: e.g., TikTok's 'for you' page. In such environments, algorithmically-driven personal selection of content, instant presentation of content, as well as interacting with the platform to 'manage' such selection is common, in contrast to media environments which users actively search for information. This might influence their easy 'acceptance' of algorithmic filtering and generate certain assumptions and knowledge with regard to algorithmic awareness, imagination and power, including a positive sense of agency.

Returning to the Gramscian theory of hegemony, and the idea that dominant ways of doing things can become so embedded that we stop questioning them, in Generation F's 'acceptance' of algorithmic filtering, the digital agency afforded may belie a wider assault on agency in more material terms. De Groot, de Haan, and van Dijken (2023, 711) continue: 'Our analyses showed that although students have a basic understanding of the working of algorithms, they did not easily translate such knowledge into how our society might be affected by, for instance, the automatic selection of information'.

It seems as if overnight social media feeds were transformed. The carefully curated list of accounts we followed suddenly played second fiddle to 'For You' feeds, that select content for us based on what we might have done rather than what we have actively chosen to do. There is a difference between a feed based on the thousands, millions, billions of traceable—yet humanly unknowable—imprints of our digital footprint, versus a feed based on that which we seemingly freely sign up and use social media platforms for. Indeed, the very structure of the internet, and the means of its accountability to citizens, has been criticised for leaving children vulnerable to opaque platform Terms and Conditions that do not meaningfully explain their functions (Vallejos et al. 2021, 3). Who agreed to this lurch towards algorithmic content selection on social media feeds? As we have suggested, above, such technological and cultural tipping points are precisely those that we did not really notice or grasp the meaning of at the time, and the mere hindsight of the passage of time does not afford any prospects of reversal, of returning to an earlier state of affairs.

Generation F, despite showing awareness of how algorithms work, risk losing sight (and oversight) over time of what algorithms work to achieve. The Gramscian theory of hegemony, applied to the relationship between young people and social media, suggests a two-fold normalisation of algorithmic empowerment. First, there is the normalisation of algorithmically selected content dominating personal feeds and, by extension, minds. Second, there follows a normalisation of the types of content, perspectives, and behaviours that these algorithms produce.

Vibes and the commodification of grief

The process of deep mediatisation pinpoints social media's embeddedness in the processes by which we conceive and store memories. The algorithm is not just innocuously drawing links between data; it is a pervasive reorientation of how and why data is produced. Brown et al. (2024) develop the concept of 'tuned' advertising to account for how algorithmically produced vibes manifest between advertisements and social media users. The 'vibe' is defined as 'the meanings, feelings, and atmospheres produced by algorithmically tuned and customized sequences of ads, not just the symbols and meanings of individual ads by themselves' (Brown et al. 2024, 2). Here, the flow or vibe between users and advertisements keeps users engaged and scrolling through content, therefore seeing a greater number of advertisements.

Users are not so much targeted by particular advertisements that may appeal to them but rather their feelings are targeted and attuned towards the vibe being curated and sold by a series of ads (Brown et al. 2024, 2). This makes it difficult for users to comprehend the ways and reasons for their being targeted. Indeed, vibes are being generated as a result of earlier algorithmically generated vibes between users, which stands to remove users further and further from any form of control over their feelings and interests. In this world, 'culture and computation are becoming less distinguishable from one another', as algorithms and those who have engineered them play an active role in drawing links between cultural outputs (Hallinan & Striphas 2016, 131).

The algorithm makes experiences opaque and difficult to trace. Crucially, a scenario ensues wherein the specific meaning or importance of individual advertisements, or content, and our relationship with them, plays second fiddle to the overarching vibe compelling us to engage with them in certain ways. The algorithm does not just recognise what we might like to buy; it senses and fine-tunes a vibe from the reasons we might want to buy it. A clear example of this process can be found by looking at how social media and algorithmically tuned internet encourages people to co-create a self, with the algorithm, that reflects trending vibes.

In her study of 'hypejacking' and the 'commodification of grief', Abidin (2022, 175) identifies a transition from our use of 'representational' to 'presentational' media (see also Lash 2002, 71) where 'users have the increasing ability to negotiate and control their public personae online' through social media. No longer a space for sharing the things that happen in our lives for our friends and families to see and react to, social media in its increasingly algorithmic form is now, for many, a space to curate, present, perform, and ultimately market a version of the self with an explicit remit: it must be a self that sells.

Social media users will be acquainted with the role of influencers, who make a living out of promoting commercial products and various marketable aesthetics and vibes within posts. At the top level of *influencing*, these forms of content promotion have been monetised, but in the contemporary social media environment, where the content of posts is secondary to the vibe they are 'giving' (Medium 2023), isn't everyone an influencer on some level? Regardless of your sphere of influence, your number of followers or the profile of your sponsors (if you have any), most social media users are in some sense influencers, reproducing algorithmic and commercial trends because of the universally applicable social media incentive to self-promote, whether for cultural or financial capital, or both.

Consider social media engagement with the explosive hashtag booms that follow disasters and tragedies. We are constantly compelled to #PrayFor someone out there, usually strangers. Whether we actually pray for them or not, or whether we ourselves are even people who pray, is irrelevant. Failure to use the hashtag is an indication of apathy or, worse yet, opposition towards its cause. But the trends are both frequent and demanding, they come as a bombardment, making it difficult to properly understand what they refer to, or to mourn the people they memorialise. After all, the important thing is that you are seen to post the hashtag, not that you have anything else to say or think about what it refers to.

This contradiction was exposed during the Black Lives Matter protests, which followed the murder of George Floyd by Minneapolis police officer, Derek Chauvin on 25 May 2020. In the wake of Floyd's murder, the Black Lives Matter movement responded with mass protest across the United States and other parts of the world. For many in Generations A and Z (collectively, Generation F), this will have been the first major digital activism movement they had experienced firsthand. On social media, the #BlackLivesMatter hashtag became a trending tag for posts of all kinds relating to ongoing events. Yet many took advantage of the trend and used it as an opportunity for self-promotion.

Rather than engage in acts of material solidarity with the movement and with Black communities, the only act was to 'show support' by sharing pictures of black squares using the #BlackLivesMatter hashtag. As a consequence of some social media influencers using the #BlackLivesMatter hashtag on posts showing black squares, people actually involved in the protest movement could not access important information online. Details of protests and useful updates from organisers were lost in a sea of black squares dominating the algorithm. Relevant communications, rather than being coordinated, were obscured by many social media and influencers' use of the hashtag, for their use of it was motivated by interests independent of the Black Lives Matter movement and its objectives. Much of the hashtag and black square solidarity from influencers was entirely performative; its core aim was to increase the influencer's own credibility with their followers (Wellman 2022).

According to Wellman (2022, 5–7), this was a missed opportunity for predominantly White 'wellness' influencers to use their platforms and significantly shift social attitudes and challenge racial inequality. Solidarity typically requires principle and some form of sacrifice, where 'the group as a whole shares the risks, burdens or possible threats' to minimise the risk of a collective threat or to defend shared values (Dawson & Verweij 2012, 1–2), yet in the case of many #BlackLivesMatter posts, these were not motivating or material factors. Influencers were quite open about the conflict Black Lives Matter presented for them, as they variably struggled to reconcile some form of support for the cause with a reluctance to alienate followers who did not support it. The issues were depoliticised with the use of infographics instead of text, proffering light platitudes in place of controversial convictions. In a well-worn '*keep politics out of ...*' approach, many attempted to separate the 'wellness' industry from political concerns, yet the two are inextricably linked. The wellness industry has long identified itself with the middle-class White experience; it is a historically racialised phenomenon (Wellman 2022, 5–7).

Some influencers engaged with Black Lives Matter by linking the accounts of Black content creators, an ostensible attempt to highlight Black voices. Yet posts used attractive fonts and branding to ensure the influencer's own platform was promoted in the process (Wellman 2022, 7). Such is the reality of political debate taking place inside spheres of commercial imperative. Wellman describes this 'meme-ification of social justice' as follows:

> Ultimately, influencers participated in performative allyship on an already performative platform, within an industry thriving through performativity. These layers of expectations regarding one's brand and oneself led to a focus on the public presentation of 'wokeness' almost

> overnight. Months later, little has changed in the wellness industry on Instagram as many influencers have returned to their original posting habits. (Wellman 2022, 8)

It is important to highlight that as a basic communicative tool, there is no reason why social media was not, or should not have been useful for building structures and capacity for meaningful solidarity during the height of the Black Lives Matter protests. In other cases, it will have been (see Lee and Ahmed 2024 for a discussion on the relationship between social media use and BLM protest participation). But clearly there are constraints on what can be achieved in such online spaces. It is difficult to build solidarity in an arena that is fundamentally geared towards self-interest.

This is the environment in which Generation F are exposed to and expected to engage with solidarity, the principles of which contrast greatly with the terms of social media and algorithmic status. Young activists and the peers they may wish to reach are wrapped up in a neoliberal media ecology that rewards commercial and self-interest, at the expense of social empowerment. As soon as the opportunity for solidarity or political education or historical reflection arises, and becomes trending, it achieves the status of a commodity; it is uprooted and repurposed for personal gain or indeed preservation. Its value has undergone a fundamental change.

The hashtag bandwagons jumped on, whether for living or dead, do not necessitate any deep consideration of those they refer to. In this new 'grief context' (Abidin 2022, 177), you cannot mourn the dead on your own watch, for your experience of mourning is tied to the fast-paced and constantly changing social media landscape where news of death occurs. Take too long to consider one tragedy, and you might miss your opportunity to 'show' you care about another.

The performative aspect of this new grief context also presents opportunities for grief to be gamed. Those savvy enough to work with the algorithm can ensure their performance of grief, their presentation of a grieving self, delivers a lucrative personal brand enhancement. From influencers marketing paid products, to microcelebrities and ordinary social media users promoting their own virtuousness, grief hashtag trends have seen public grieving commodified and turned into 'publicity grieving' (Abidin 2022, 175). At the level of the ordinary person, we might join in to demonstrate an aspect of our personality, by showing we are aware of and endorse the latest collective acknowledgement of tragedy. On a more cynical level, influencers apply trending hashtags to their paid posts to bump them up the algorithmic trend. In both cases, the publicity gained through public performances of grief is more important than not only grieving on a genuine level (for who can possibly grieve and mourn on a deep level for all of these tragedies at once?) but also becomes more of a motivation than the actual processes of grieving, mourning, and coming to terms with death.

And what of the demonstration itself? What, materially, does posting hashtags actually achieve? While the merits of digital activism, or 'slacktivism', are the subject of debate (Lane & Cin 2017, Cabrera et al. 2017, Lee & Ahmed 2024), our point here rather concerns a shifting conceptualisation of solidarity, and by extension, reality. If the central measurement of someone's solidarity—the one with the greatest consequences for their reputation and the value of their 'self'—is their contribution to a hashtag trend, does this not suggest a supremacy for the virtual over the material, the artificial over the authentic, the performative over the demonstrative?

No time like the lonely (neoliberal) present

According to Statista, in 2024, the UK had 56.2 million active social media users, notably 82.8% of the British population (Statista 2025a). Across neoliberal, or 'post-neoliberal' Western societies, our use of social media forms an important role in the conditioning and cultivating of ourselves. In a study of Swedish social media users, Bengtsson and Johansson (2022) found three prominent types of everyday use. There are the times we use social media to alter our mood, the times we use it ritually to engage with the world (for example, first thing in the morning and last thing at night, not unlike mass media engagement prior to the invention of the smartphone), and finally, the times we use social media to fill empty slots of time. Collectively, these categories are quite comprehensive; they suggest that basically we use our phones all the time. However, it is the third category in particular that speaks to the character of the neoliberal 'soul' (discussed in Chapter 2). Bengtsson and Johansson found in their study that,

> The respondents described [using social media to fill empty slots of time] as a kind of un-reflected use, where the content is subordinate to the purpose of killing time and keeping loneliness away. This kind of interval use is hence experienced as tech-independent, it is not most important which platform they use in the temporal interstices—instead it is the purpose of fighting monotony and social emptiness that gives it meaning. (Bengtsson and Johansson 2022, 6)

Here, meaning comes from clicking on or consuming content, not the actual content itself. If it is a distraction from the present, where you may be alone with nothing to do but reflect, then it is fit for purpose. It seems that we cannot stand the discomfort that comes with silence. The neoliberal present, after all, is a lonely place; its challenges are there for you alone to contend with. This is not to say that loneliness is a new thing, although the type and severity of collective loneliness we experience in neoliberal society is quite profound in scale, with chatbots taking the place of real interactions due to a systemic assault on the presence of third spaces for socialising (Cantor 2024). But beyond loneliness, or perhaps at the root of it, is a compulsion to consume distraction content regardless of its value, so long as it *holds* one's attention in order to *divert* one's attention from whatever is happening in front of them, or their thoughts on what might happen later, or did happen yesterday.

The deeper problems in life are too complex to solve, and we do not have enough time to solve them. Indeed, capitalism has systemically made it so, by structuring life with layers of stress, disempowerment, and isolation. Alienated from any sense of shared class interest, and the capacity to wield it, we retreat into the comfort of the distraction, the entertainment, so readily available and always there. The system, on the one hand, drives a wedge between us and the world, yet on the other hand, puts the entire world in our pocket, not to give us more options but to distract us from understanding how few we truly have (Pilkington 2024).

For Generation F (Forget), this amounts to a significant reorientation of memory itself, an end to memory as we once knew it, replaced with a dependency on technology for memories and to produce new—and highly fragmented—ones. The contemporary space for communication and consumption, our smartphones and social media, at once plays on and increases our cognitive and emotional compulsion to consume content whose remit is, above all else, to distract us.

The battle between authenticity and entertainment as units of value is perhaps nowhere more evident than the celebrity influencer boxing circuit. Tom Usher (2024) rightly blames a 'cultural economy that rewards attention and engagement over artistry and skill' for the rise of boxing bouts between random celebrities where 'it doesn't matter how good [they] are at fighting—as long as its "good content," nobody cares'. In other words, as long as it holds our ever-shrinking attention span (Duffy and Thain 2022), it is of value. The amount of time, energy, and thought it might take someone to learn enough about the sport of boxing to appreciate professional contests over these gimmicky, fiery, low-quality celebrity bouts, ultimately amounts to a lesser value.

The gamification of memory

In this context, the definition and importance of the 'real' is starting to change. At the very least, AI is being used to augment and transcend experiences that until now were the preserve of human beings. Artist and designer Refik Anadol uses GAN algorithms to generate 'synesthetic reality experiments ... [turning] datasets into latent multi-sensory experiences to commemorate the beauty of the earth we share' (Anadol 2021). His 2021 *Nature Dreams* installation asked whether machines, much like they are able to learn, can also dream and hallucinate. Through 'the lens of nature aesthetics', we are invited to consider whether AI can 'not only mimic reality but imagine beyond it'. Anadol uses AI to not only replicate a human experience but also move beyond it and create something more profound in its place.

In a 2023 installation titled *Artificial Realities: Coral*, Anadol uses AI to create an underwater virtual reality, one of coral unspoiled by human interference and abstracted with the profound imagination of his AI. One day, scientists might be able to use AI to 3D-print new coral to replace that which has been destroyed by human beings (Kurcfeld 2024). Here, the potential of Anadol's AI goes a step further; his is a future where AI dreams for us and has the power to replace that which is lost in our natural world. In a TED Talk from 2023, Anadol himself admits that 'one day, we might be only left with the simulations of corals in a virtual world' (Anadol 2023). In this scenario, the only coral that exists is an AI-generated and aggregated rendition of coral as it was up until its extinction in the real world; its evolutionary process stops, as does our capacity to learn from it in its real and present form. Anadol goes on to discuss a collaborative project with indigenous Amazonian rainforest communities, whose ancient knowledge and ways of remembering their local natural world is being mapped onto an open-source generative AI 'that can even reconstruct extinct flora and fauna' (Anadol 2023).

To take this step by step: First, there is the AI that dreams and hallucinates from the perspective of nature, ultimately transcending the bounds of human imagination. Then, there is the AI that creates a virtual version of nature currently vanishing from our present, and finally, there is the AI that attempts to create a virtual version of nature that is a feature of our past. Collectively, these projects invite us to consider the merits of a natural world that exists artificially yet ostensibly provides a greater depth of knowledge of nature as it currently exists or, crucially, as we collectively remember it. This is a world where stories, memories, and experiences are more than the sum of their parts. Removed from their contextual and localised basis, aggregated and then reimagined by the machine, they offer a more profound insight, for they offer something that never really existed in this form at all. Reconstructed artificial corals are based on a rendering of five billion images of previously existing coral. Extinct plants are reimagined by loading ancient collective memories into an immensely powerful generative AI. The resulting insights may well offer commercial, cultural, and scientific value, and may even be accurate in their cosmetic makeup, yet, they remain the hallucinations of a machine. Does the meaning of the past really need to be transcended rather than simply understood? On the risk of environmental memory being constructed from the abstract perspective of AI rather than the material, humanly lived world, Morehouse (2025, 6) argues:

> If the past recedes because ecological contexts have changed or because AI is generating hallucinations by invoking non-existent events, the dislocation of environmental memory from its constitutive *where* undermines the capacity to mobilise memory to avert future catastrophe .... This empties meaning of its transformative potential.

The generative capacity of AI stirs up considerable debate over the meaning of authenticity, truth, and fact. Increasingly, AI is being used to generate artefacts, which show us 'what something would be like' in a series of unverifiable circumstances. In February 2024, the *New York Post* published an article titled, 'Jack the Ripper's face finally revealed— here's what AI thinks the notorious prostitute killer looked like' (Landsel 2024). The article shows an AI-generated image of a man based on 'information' and photographs of relatives of one of the prime suspects for Jack the Ripper's identity in the late-1800s. His identity was not confirmed at the time, but nonetheless, the AI purports to expose or 'reveal' something new about him to us. The AI model is applied to bring pre-existing human-generated theories to life. While critical audiences can perhaps choose whether to deem this kind of content to be useful or gimmicky, it is an issue that they are being asked to do so. Verifiable or scientifically produced historical revelations risk being confused with 'fun' AI content. Rather than performing a consolidating methodological role in the study of history, AI models here are producing distortion and ambiguity.

A growing trend in the AI generation of video transforms still paintings or images of historical figures into motion, and seemingly ever closer to some kind of *reality*. The importance of uncovering more of material history and analysing it from the perspective of our present is trumped by a chance to 'reveal' more about their 'true' appearance. After all, this is the primary means by which we learn about and value our modern celebrities; why not use AI to apply the same logic to Vincent van Gogh?

Another example, Upscaling History is a website and YouTube channel that uses AI to 'clone' speeches made by historical political figures and translate them into another language (Upscaling History 2024a). It is not just a translation tool, however, as AI clones the voice characteristics of the speaker, to let us hear how they themselves would sound if they were from X country. 'What Would Hitler Have Sounded Like in English?' (Upscaling History 2024b) purports to show us how Hitler's voice would sound if he were a native English speaker. The video description professes that 'state of the art' AI is used to 'preserve the accents, language, and motion' displayed by Hitler and other political figures.

The claim around accent preservation requires further scrutiny. Upscaling History does not make it clear how Hitler's accent has been 'preserved' in their 'cloned' interpretation of him in English. He appears to have an upper-class South-England accent that sometimes sounds slightly American, although we can expect that the technology will improve in time and present something more consistent. The issue is, while generalisations can be made based on Hitler's social class status in Austria and Germany, and the most common English accents found in British politics, Upscaling History is taking a massive leap in claiming that this is how Hitler would have sounded in English and by extension, if he himself were English. This is rather a presumptuous and unscientific cloning process, which risks positing a hugely reductive portrayal of Hitler (or any historical political figure), their social class background and many other cultural idiosyncrasies captured in their speech, accent, and mannerisms. There is a risk that, in satisfying the hypothetical, Upscaling History revises the actual, with a muddying impact for truth and reality.

Furthermore, while Upscaling History is a relatively small project very much in its infancy—with 7.14K YouTube channel subscribers—its video clips are being shared far and wide on social media, without much critique of their veracity or scientific composition. Other, similar voice cloning projects are operating at the same time, with entirely different results. For example, the same short clip of a Hitler speech has been translated/cloned into English using another AI (Unknown, YouTube 2024), and 'Hitler' sounds completely different.

The market for this type of application of AI, one focused on a reimagined and deepened celebrity fakery of historical figures, is very on-brand in our era of vapid distraction media. This trend, of using technology to gamify rather than demystify, is just another example of neoliberalism's assault on the conditions for new cultural production—its war on our capacity to mount a challenge to its cultural hegemony. It seems we are entering a period where the past is fetishised, uncanny, and there to distract from the present: 'Entropy is the enemy of speedy consumption, since it may induce confusion, rejection or a pause for thought. It seems, then, that as in Flusser's nightmare vision of eternal boredom, these monopolists are selling us a terminal sense of déjà vu' (Stallabrass 2024).

A similar example in 2024 saw late comedian George Carlin's family take legal action against podcast outlet *Dudesy* for their AI-generated comedy special of 'Carlin' delivering material on current events (Associated Press 2024). The deepfake—created without the permission of Carlin's estate—violated copyright in its rendering of George Carlin's (who died in 2008) comedic perspective on events that he was not alive to experience. This is a different example of AI being used to show us what would have been to the Hitler or Jack the Ripper content described above. These AI artefacts endeavour to enrich our understanding of how historical figures were at the time they were alive, showing us previously unknown or impossible-to-determine aspects.

In the case of the George Carlin AI special, the George Carlin of a specific time period, his personality, knowledge, and style at that time, is being transported into a completely new era. Thus, not only is a new memory of Carlin created—in that the AI delivers 'new material'—but a new George Carlin is created, one who sees contemporary events through the lens of someone who only knew the world pre-2008. Had Carlin been alive today, there is no way of knowing who he would have been or what his material would have been like, with the benefit of 17 more years on Earth. AIs like these usher in a post-authentic cultural epoch, where the real cultural, political, and philosophical phenomena of bygone eras are replayed and distorted to satisfy the vapid (post-) cultural demands of an era and perhaps a generation somewhat content with virtual and mimicked experiences.

What should a comedian be like today? What makes good comedy and commentary today? Is it to do with finding groundbreaking forms and spaces for originality, or is it about successfully marketing comedy that rehashes and reimagines the originality of yore and projects it onto the present, entertaining (distracting) us with silliness rather than inviting us to assess its quality?

Perhaps the answer is complicated. There is a thriving stand-up comedy scene in the UK, and performers can differentiate between the art of their routines and the content they produce 'clips' of to sell tickets online (Christopher Macarthur-Boyd discusses this on the *Here Comes The Guillotine* podcast). Artists are clearly able to game social media and algorithms, enticing audiences with a digital dopamine hit in the hope that they might then invest in the prospect of a real-life and far more sophisticated experience. This is evidence that 'creators' are not simply lapsing to the virtual world's lull, instead they are able to capitalise on its absurdities to deliver benefits in the real world. Yet it is telling that online clippable content plays such an important role in the marketing of 'real' content that exists outside the game.

Fell, Tan, and Kyd's (2024) Inside TikTok's Money Machine is an ABC feature article about the addictive nature of TikTok—for both users and influencers—and how the app facilitates the monetisation of boredom and distraction content. Yet, ironically, the article itself is formatted as a kind of game where you must scroll to reveal more shiny content and graphics instead of standard text. Perhaps there is no irony here at all, and the article simply takes note of the fact that its target audience, TikTok users, would not stick around to read the full thing unless it was presented as some kind of game with dopamine rewards for every slight scroll. Unable to read an article, we instead need to play it, doing as we read, multi-tasking, engaging, and being distracted, our focus contingent on a constant compulsion to get, see, and click more. From stand-up comedians selling their art to broadcasters selling the news, the impulse for instant gratification first, serious stuff second, is real. This impulse to reduce art and media to soundbites is driven by the algorithmic and cognitive demand for instant gratification.

The clickbaiting of the past—the ultimate gamification of memory—has arrived. And just like the digital self, as long as it captures attention, it is saleable under the social and technological conditions that preclude contemplation in favour of instant gratification, that reward performance over substance, and that replace authenticity and originality with imitation. The construction of and relationship to the self in this environment is, as we have shown, one that reflects the commodified, fragmented, and precarious character of neoliberal society. And memory, both in the head and in the wild, is transformed.

5
The Digital Fusion of Head and Wild

Mind the gap

An extensive amount of scholarly research has been conducted into the workings of the human mind and memory processing. This interrogates exactly how we as individual humans remember and what types of memories we tend to prioritise (Hamilton & Benjamin 2019, Marsh & Rajaram 2019). Work also targets the physiological and structural changes that different mnemonic aids and pathways of remembering shape within our brain's architecture (Bjork & Bjork 1988, Risko 2019). Polemics on the generation of false memories and the general distortion of reality within the remembered (and, by proxy, also the unremembered) world have been at the centre of intrigue generated by this field (Mitchell & Thompson 1994, Lanier 2010, Shaw 2020, Lewandowsky & Pomerantsev 2021, Rajaram 2024, Evans & Rigato 2024, Tay & Ecker 2024, Murphy, Egan & Greene 2024).

We contribute to these debates through focusing on the relationship between memory and the complex and politicised digital ecology that shapes it, to help bridge the gap between social and human science approaches to memory studies and questions of how memory has reached its present juncture. Much of the existing literature has been framed, rather inevitably, in the context of the technological progress society has experienced in the late twentieth and early twenty-first century (Geiger 2014, Alvarado & Waern 2018, Russell 2019, Storm 2019). There is no escaping the inclusion of (or downright focus on) the digital world and media in the debate on what is noticed, what is emphasised, and what is retained from the world around us, in today's digital memory ecology.

The AI Memory Machine. Andrew Hoskins, Kristína Čimová, and Danny Pilkington,
Oxford University Press.
DOI: 10.1093/oso/9780198995906.003.0005

The problematic part of thinking about memory in relation to the human brain vis à vis the internet and digital media comes when we try to separate memory itself from its source. Even without the use and need for technology, humans are prone to creating and sustaining false memories (Shaw 2020) or recalling events in less than realistic light, for example, by recollecting them more fondly than truthfully (also known as the effect of rosy retrospection) (Mitchell & Thompson 1994).

Furthermore, the particular potency and difficulty with memory as facilitated or quashed by digital media, lies in the lack of empathy that algorithmic recall provides (Shaw 2015). Some memories should be buried or lost but frequently digital and AI devices and services retrieve and remake them for us, approximating them through targeted advertising, or shared through social media networks (Shaw 2015). This is a concept explored in literature elsewhere, raising the valid question of digital media platforms such as Facebook's 'On This Day' preventing 'healthy and necessary forgetting' (Hoskins 2011) and facilitating entrapment in a world where you may have to face your ex-partners or friends or painful/humiliating situations endlessly (Lanier 2010). How many times have we seen a celebrity or a friend share their memory as suggested by the social media outlet with a 'Can't believe it's been a year already' or a variation thereof? What is the purpose or the value of such an exercise for both the author and posterity?

Having established that the involvement of technology in memory generation and sustainability may affect not just our emotions but cognitive processes themselves (Marsh & Rajaram 2019), we are also concerned with exploring whether digital media function as memory aids and portals (Hoskins 2011) or whether they in fact *become* memory itself. To what extent, in other words, are we able to separate our memory from the visualisation provided by Facebook for this memory? To what extent does such a memory carry meaning for us in the way it was originally captured? Shaw, for instance, states that this is a real problem for our minds, as we are likely to forget related and unmentioned information within a memory that we take a snapshot of, to share on Facebook (Shaw 2015). Therefore, while we may be comfortable with remembering a particular situation, for example, an evening during a holiday, we may forget who we went with, where it took place, what we felt, and how we took in our surroundings before and after the memory was immortalised.

This problem is akin to the concept of flashbulb memory (FBM) (Brown & Kulik 1977, Hoskins 2009), which describes human memory that can apparently be recalled vividly as though reproduced from the original event and of 'photographic' quality. FBM has also been found to be largely inaccurate in reality and compiled from several sources, much like the work on the creation of false autobiographical memories shows (Loftus & Pickrell 1995, Jou & Flores 2013), where the person accessing their false memory believes they are accessing a real memory. Such warping of memories is in effect a form of forgetting, and digital media are instrumental in how this process takes place for the born-digital generation.

Shaw states that this forgetting effect is ever more likely to deepen, the more a particular memory is rehashed. In other words, the rehashing facilitated by Facebook or Instagram is increasing the potential of distorting the memory itself in its very core (Shaw 2015). We must then, as a moral imperative, speak of the digital ecosystem not as separate from, but as part of, life in its rawest form, integrated within our very ability to construct identity as based on our lived experiences and our ability to experience nostalgia or learn from such experiences. If memory itself is warped, isn't the lesson learnt equally as warped? It is vital that we consider the impacts of a commodified and distorted reality, all of which reframe our thinking on memory in a way that is driven by external, structural influences that did not originate in our minds, but which are now inextricable from them, and inescapable.

Memory accuracy

Within the concept of reality and memory construction, we are necessarily faced with the accuracy dilemma. People tend to think of social media and internet features as possessive of personality and accuracy. It is now normal for our phones to greet us with a cheery 'Good morning, [insert name]' from a social media platform, count our calorie intake, track our sleep and our physical activity, and remind us to make sure we drink enough water and send a message to our friend on their birthday.

The platforms and digital technology generally instil confidence in their knowledge and in their accuracy. However, as Hamilton and Benjamin (2019) point out, the internet is indifferent towards accuracy and relative permanence. It is still up to humans to be able to infer what is 'true' of the world, and this is our main strength in a world of digital and media technology. Whereas the internet prefers data and information and the accumulation of it, combined with access and availability, the human mind prioritises inference and making sense of information (Hamilton & Benjamin 2019). We should therefore be seeking to establish coherence where the internet cannot or will not do so. This applies to memory as well.

However, the internet, digital and AI driven media, and social networks intervene in the production of coherence in self and memory over time. For example, the rehashing of memories prevents our innate ability to forget in an evolutionary manner. A lot of the time, the brain forgets and discards out-of-date information, for example, to make it easier to retrieve current and relevant information (Bjork & Bjork 1988). Yet, the digital (memory) ecology concerns itself only with an accumulation of information and presents in search queries the information that is most searched for and accessible, not what is most accurate, relevant, or current (Hamilton & Benjamin 2019). This is why shopping sites have the functions of 'filter by' and 'sort by': 'bestsellers', 'most relevant to search', 'newest', and so on. And the potential to search through our own memories, not simply altered, but a lot of the time directly generated by the digital ecosystem, is a fantasy increasingly being realised by technologists and through AI imaginaries.

Markham and Pereira (2019) find that algorithms use their own premade categories to flatten and retrofit lived memory into the logic outlined by data models. The question arising from this is not the ethics of the present but that of the future—what possible futures are being 'enabled' or 'disabled' by such manipulation of memories (Markham & Pereira 2019)? By constraining memory within the logic of an algorithm (whose design is guided by a social and political base), accuracy is assumed to exist within these confines too.

Marsh and Rajaram (2019) point out that some information sources actively try to convince the reader of their accuracy by making information more attractive and/or memorable. This is also why conspiracy theories gain a lot of traction online—it has been shown that fake but scandalous and attractive news spreads faster than real news (Roberts 2016). Accuracy and reality therefore become subject to our own design, by searching for things in specific ways, validating memory sharing in particular ways, or repeatedly relying on similar websites. By this creation of a pattern, algorithms are fed and a sort of Einstellung (mental autopilot) effect takes place (Luchins 1942).

In digital terms, this becomes a meta circle of viciousness, where we are no longer able to discern the reality of memory, which in turn constructs our identity (Storm 2019). Confluence of the external and internal information in this manner is inevitable, which leads to the logical question: if *my own* thoughts and thoughts generated *for me* conflate, then are my memories just enhanced or are they directly generated by algorithms? If the algorithm learns from our way of searching for material, it follows that it affects the way we search in the future. Equally then, if it has affected our way of searching for (and absorbing) information, does it not rid us entirely of the ability to create or perceive original memory by a perpetual cycle of pre-determination?

Taking this one step further by including the agency of digital media and social media in the equation, a set of variables other than just accuracy present themselves, such as memory storage and access, speed of memory recall, and, perhaps most importantly: the value assigned to personal *and* collective memories. These factors will inevitably impact what is remembered on a general level, but what is likely to be remembered of the present in the future once all these filters are applied?

Our most mundane communicational acts are archival; we scatter digital traces of ourselves just through being social, through working, or even by doing nothing, information pours out of our smartphones as we sleep. So, whereas media audiences had collective anonymity in their media consumption of the twentieth century, in today's digital memory ecology, it is users that are made personally accountable. The prospects of aspects of your life, acts, and traces, emerging at unpredictable times in the future, are massively increased, and you have little or no control over how this might happen. We put it all out there, but we cannot really take it back.

As a result, there has been a shift in how individuals are remembered in society. Moving from the comparatively unrecorded self to the immensely over recorded self, the wider anonymity that comes with only being known through human social connections is vanishing.

On the one hand, the ability of each person to create their own memories leads to a situation in which there is no shared memory, as every individual has their own smartphone photo roll. This is part of the technologically driven growing individualisation of memory. And yet on the other hand, there is a massification of memory at an astonishing scale. Billions of individuals routinely and often instantly post and share their photos and videos on apps and platforms. This includes new forms of proprietorial memories—designed, stored, algorithmically ordered, prompted, owned but also erased by private companies and those that exploit and control social media platforms. Participation in modern society compels us to use technologies that at once hyper-individualise our memories and forfeit control of them to the platforms providing such an outsource.

There is a new battleground of memory, around who has the right to remember and to forget, in a world in which we increasingly and often willingly overproduce the self. Everyday and profound acts of digital communication and the forging of connections feel lively and under our control with the comfort of immediacy, yet in this newfound utility lies a diminished consciousness of media's impact in the long term.

Ultimately, digital existence weakens what was once an active memory, a human memory that had to work hard to sustain a continuity of past—of identity, of place, of relationships—with the shift from reliance to dependency on the search devices of our machines.

What will be memorable and accessible and meaningful of digital memory, in say 20 years from now is difficult to predict. One of our expert interviewees, Jacob Appel, an algorithmic auditor, poses this same question:

> I think it's going to be a stream of memes. It's going to be a quick slideshow of memes. I don't think they're going to fit together. I don't

> think that memory, in this information environment, I don't think that it's really tuned towards narrative or connection between things.[1]

Similarly, on the website for memory app *1 Second Everyday*, a user is quoted as saying: 'This app is like a memory of your life flashing before your eyes'. Is this what digital memory will become, overloaded, always in motion, always sampled, without any time for pause, reflection, and a complete fragmentation of the social past? With technology able to edit, distort, mesh, and speed things up, are we at risk of being left behind? Memory in the head can be complicated, evolving, and hard to sort out. Why bother when digital and AI devices can do the hard work for you?

This idea is perpetuated by app and smartphone designers. The Google Pixel smartphone, for example, promotes the idea of taking a photo and tapping on all that you would like to disappear from the image, which the phone will then erase and replace with predicted content of background. The manufacturer captures this with the slogan: 'It's perfect. Just like your memories. And how you want to remember them'. It is a frightening concept to think that what is being promoted here is a removal of all that is naturally present in a memory to produce an airbrushed, Instagram-ready image of memory without any imperfections.

What will be the effect of this endeavour on our memories? Will memories that are curated, deliberately altered, and promoted indefinitely change who we are? If so, what will be the result of this process? As is our claim, for Generation F(orget), the immediate impact is that memory-making processes no longer identify with those experienced by preceding generations.

Two types of forgetting

Most of individual experience prior to the age of AI was captured in media that were fairly predictable in their lifespan (their 'decay time', Hoskins 2013) and therefore so was the dissipation of recorded memory of a given society. This allows us to identify two principal forms of forgetting.

The first mode of forgetting is that if experiences or events are never 'encoded' into memory, that is, in media memory, in the first place. For instance, even by the late twentieth century, much of human everyday experience was never actually recorded or documented at all, being too trivial, too traumatic, or too private. And the recording of life usually involved planning and effort.

The second form of forgetting occurs when things that have been articulated, recorded, or documented, held in memory, eventually fade or decay, or are lost, displaced, or erased. Historically, most media forms rotted, yellowed, faded, and flickered, becoming inevitably obscure and obsolete. It seems odd then that much of the latter part of the twentieth century is associated with a 'memory boom' (Winter 2017), given these conditions of the general unencoding of memory and of media decay.

In the digital era, however, the first form of forgetting, at least, appears in retreat. It seems that very little of human experience is unrecorded. Driven by the pervasiveness and convenience of the smartphone, there now occurs an overproduced self, distributed and remembered through digital connectivity. Each individual, therefore, requires an over-connectivity, an over-reliance on recording and sharing the private and mundane moments not only of their own but also of other people's lives, to drive engagement with, and validation of, their own (self). You capture, often without consent, a moment passing in the life of a friend, relative, or stranger. You have identified meaning in that moment, a caption, a way to frame that moment for the benefit of those who upon interacting with your caption will identify with the same meaning, identify with you. And the moment itself, the significant, private, mundane, remembered, or forgotten occurrence in the life of that friend, relative, or stranger, becomes a part of you, a part of the self that you have participated in producing.

Furthermore, beyond that which we deliberately produce, our basic everyday communicational acts are archival. The digital traces we consciously and unconsciously produce are stored and analysed. At multiple levels and in multiple ways, then, the individual is targeted, exposed, revealed, surveilled, and datafied. And the processes of surveillance and algorithmic identification produce, or 'remember' versions of ourselves that are unknown, unrecognisable, and indeed unremembered by us as individuals. Our human minds could not possibly remember, therefore comprehend, the 'self' created through every single datafied action we take.

Algorithmically, you are known, and commercially exploited, for being a person who tends to buy X type of milk, look at Y type of social media content, search for Z type of health issue, spend time in V type of bar, and millions, even billions of other variables, all of which combine to remember you and map out what you might do next in ways that you do not even know yourself. Over time, what are the implications of having a 'you' owned by Big Tech and projected on to *you* every minute of the day? When you find yourself now looking at a new type of social media content, is this because you sought it out, or because 'you' might like to see it, and then decide to buy a new type of milk?

For many, the ostensible utility of being known by an algorithm will outweigh the cost of being slowly drained of agency. Yet for those it does not, for those who want to go back to being sold *to* rather than sold, how is it possible to hide and be 'forgotten'? As we have discussed, even the European legislation on the Right to Be Forgotten (RtbF) cannot temper such extreme exposure. And as Szakolczai (2023, 6) finds, in his ethnographic account of an attempt to resist online capture, the cost of 'not being allowed a proper [web] navigation experience' and the 'annoyance' of peers who sensed a 'parasitic' feature in using someone else's tech because you do not own your own, it is very difficult and even harmful to try and remain hidden. The first principal form of being forgotten, through experience never recorded or documented in the first place, seems to be vanishing, and along with it, a fundamental right.

But the datafication of the self and of experience also upends the second form of forgetting, the one that occurs through media decay. Who can possibly predict the finitude of the ravaging of personal data, algorithmic processing, metadata, and the general tagging of life? Societies now wrestle with the uses and abuses of humans' expansive digital trails, and our capacity to shape, edit, own, and restrict them. Remembering and forgetting are fought over on the battlefield of personal data and media content. The commercial value of datafied society is of such significance that we cannot reasonably expect media decay without transformative systemic overhaul. Yet with the memory feed and its constant reproduction of capitalist ideals, the prospects for such change are wrapped up and diluted by every reaffirming swirl of capitalism's cultural hegemony.

Digital technologies, media, networks, and archives therefore utterly transform both forms of traditional forgetting: (1) the absence of recording (and potentially encoding) into memory, and (2) the decline and decay of that which has been recorded. We are left with what we have called the memory feed, an overproduction of the self and of the past, fed through a digital and algorithmic nudging of individuals to record and share data and media content.

The memory feed is a process of a constant flux in the relationship between the individual, their production of data and content about themselves and their experiences, the design and uses of the platforms and apps that gather, and how these learn from and nudge users to capture, produce, and share more of their experiences in new ways. For instance, one of our expert interviewees, Cesar Kuriyama, said that 'a lot of our memories don't have a form yet',[2] suggesting that digital tech has considerable potential to offer precisely new shape and presence to our memories. These new ways include the imagination of designers to explore the multiple possibilities in which our data trails can come to be gathered, collated, and re-imagined as a form of memory. We can trace this shift by looking at the evolution of the *Timehop* app:

> One of our earliest prototypes literally pulled your text messages from a year ago and showed you your old text messages. We were scraping those out of your phone. We looked into getting credit card transactions. Every year at tax season when I'm going through my records of all my expenses, it's just this nostalgic trip down memory lane. I'm like, "How did I spend $100? Oh yes, that was a great restaurant. That was a great night." The initial idea was we would pull your MetroCard transactions on the subway. We'd pull credit cards transactions too. We'd pull background location tracking from your phone. We'd pull Strava rides, Strava bike rides. Runkeeper runs. We'd collect everything, all of your digital debris, your digital footprints and then showcase them through this one day at a time with a one year delay. (Jonathan Wegener, memory app designer and co-founder of *Timehop*)[3]

In this way, the potential for memory becomes highly personalised and individualised. The overproduction of the self in this way challenges ideas around the digital's establishment of more collective or social versions of the past.

Thus, as the traditionally established two types of forgetting are vanishing, in their place arrives a re-imagined potential for memory altogether. As Wegener usefully puts it: 'it's no longer a shared, collective, singular memory. It's a disparate, individualised, deeper version of memories because everyone has their own digital media'.[4] Yet, at the same time, the fact that so many other individuals, organisations, and platforms are also part of a generalised overproduction of the past, there are many more possibilities for connecting, mapping, and integrating the scattered data and media content from others.

Wegener explains the process of this thinking in his development of *Timehop*:

> We got really interested in how we can build automatic logging solutions in a diary feature so that in a year's time you have more memories and better memories. Even if you didn't take a photo, can we collect the photos from around you? We prototyped something that, for example, if you're standing in a restaurant or a bar, the photos that get posted in that bar on Instagram during the time period where you're there, not by you, but someone else's photos magnetically stick to you. The idea was, as you're navigating around the world in Magneto mode, the photos are magnetically attaching to you. The news events, the things that are happening around you that might have been looking at or seeing or watching, even if you took no photos, collect into an archive that is hopefully relevant to what you experience[5].

Individuals routinely remember and use the past by intertwining personal experiences with public events. Personal experiences are thereby framed through the larger apertures of shared events, and psychologists have long been interested in exploring the 'where were you when' question, to test for the accuracy or otherwise of human memory in relation to momentous events. But with the memory feed, news of the self and news of the world are both potentially sticky in memory, minable, and representable together into a unifying experience of memory of that time. Nothing is forgotten, but more than that, your memory comprises not just your experiences but the experiences of others. Memory both in the head and in the wild of other people becomes part of your own!

Cesar Kuriyama, CEO of *1 Second Everyday*, told us that one of the original visions for his company was to 'build a collective journal of humanity', to offer an astonishing social visual record of a particular day across the world. However, he explained that their experimentation with a series of videos geotagged around the world in a day, did not take off: 'People seem to care about their own videos or videos of their friends and family. But [not] when it's a mishmash of people they have no connection with. Any video I ever posted, the comments were just people saying like "02:45, that's me." They only cared about it [as though] it was almost a treasure hunt: "Did my video make it? I want to know I'm in there"'.[6]

Self, identity and autobiographical memory

Immersion in the digital memory ecology increasingly compels people to construct their own identity within its parameters of exchange of access to and use of digital and AI services. This has profound implications for how the self is conceptualised and valued. Because, to succeed in this systemically commodified setting, the self like any other commodity must be one that sells.

The American psychotherapist and psychological theorist, Carl Rogers (1967, 232–237) argued that we experience greater contentment and happiness the more our perceived self is congruent with our 'ideal' self. In other words, for Rogers, the more we feel we are who we wish we were, the happier we are. A person's capacity to achieve this level of congruence, and to assert some degree of agency and confidence over their self-perception, personhood, and material circumstances, is shaped by the impact of social structural influences in their lives. The self is therefore a product of the interaction between persons and social forces (Callero 2014, 276).

In this century, this relationship is rendered increasingly contingent on human–human, human–machinic, and machinic–machinic entanglements (Makhortykh 2024) afforded through smart devices, apps, and platforms. Qi Wang (2022) for example, in her influential 'triangular theory of self' in the social media era, argues that the self comprises three key forms of 'representations'. These are, the 'private' representation of the self in the mind, the 'registered' self as externalised and shared on digital platforms in the wild, and an 'inferred' sense of self, as a collectively constituted response through making meaning out of responses (and their absence) in our digital feeds (Wang 2022). Wang (2022) further argues that these forms of representation 'mutually influence each other via dynamic, interactive, and transactive processes', but with autobiographical memory as central in this forging of selfhood and identity.

A pre-digital version of the forging of individual memory through representing ourselves to ourselves and to others is the idea of the 'remembered self', through which emotion and memory are linked (Singer & Salovey 1993). Singer and Salovey take 'narrative memory' (1993, 216) as central to the forging of the remembered self. There is a history to this form of externalisation of memory (see Chapter 2) and the massive expansion of the capacity of individual human remembering through what Donald calls 'symbolic technologies' which 'liberate consciousness from the limitations of the brain's biological memory systems' (2002, 305).

Donald, Singer and Salovey, and Wang's important human science accounts of how human memory is shaped in its sharing, telling, and retelling have in common a mostly optimistic view of the head–wild relationship, and the stability of self-identity through these autobiographical underpinnings. And today, the processes of cognition and memory in the head are availed new potential in the digital wild. Wang (2024, 15), explains, 'This new way of remembering and sharing personal experiences is unprecedented in human history. It has essentially revolutionized memory expression and communication, creating a tangible online extension of autobiographical memory with infinite possibilities'. Just think of the sheer scale of the number of images, videos, messages, produced, posted, and scattered over a digital lifetime, that today can be said to be constitutive of your being in the world, of your infinitely sharable autobiographical memory.

The AI memory machine is an accelerant, magnifier, and distributor of the self's memorial presence. But it is also a hacker, thief, seller, and ultimately the new keeper of your memory. In the algorithmically charged archive of social media, there is a shift to *auto*-biographical memory. This renders the trajectory of what today's past will be and our place within it, hugely uncertain. Sure, there is a feeling of agency and control in our sense of the visible and active sharing of ourselves and experiences on social media. But this is also entangled with a memory of and by the self that is produced through our connectivity and dependency on services and apps that bleed in largely opaque ways, personal and very personal information about ourselves.

A first mode of auto-biographical memory then is the one identified in Wang's (2022, 2024) excellent work, the visible sense of our public presentation, sharing, and hiding of ourselves in and from the full glare of the digital ecology, although aided and abetted by the affordances of platforms. The second mode is the comparatively silent revolution in data and its AI-shaped forms that automate versions of ourselves as datapoints, as individuals subject to surveillance, as fodder for companies to profit from helping us to shape ourselves in our own image (see Chapter 2).

These two modes of auto-biographical memory in their layering and scattering of the self, together, shape an individual's stickiness in the world and resilience to not being forgotten. Auto-biographical memory differs then from autobiographical memory in that rather than the idea of narration (above), in the telling of stories about us, which fosters a stable sense of self, has been hijacked. The liberating 'symbolic technologies' of representation that Donald (2002) wrote of, have in effect performed a reversal. They instead interweave the individual with a past that they have in part made, yes, but also one given up to the vagaries of the net, making the self newly accountable and requiring near constant attention and care.

Consider, for example, the ways in which the founding of personal and intimate new relationships is shared through digital participation. New relationships are either 'hard launched' (formally confirmed and committed to) or 'soft launched' (alluded to) in social media posts that follow unspoken yet universally acknowledged rules of distinction (Hebert 2023). When users 'soft launch' their new relationship, they might post a silhouette or partial image of their partner that does not reveal their full identity. This reassures their partner of a seriousness in their commitment, without putting the relationship under the kind of strain that comes with public exposure. Furthermore, 'posting [hard launching] someone too early in the relationship could spell disaster, and scrubbing an ex from your social media can oftentimes be a painstaking process' (Hebert 2023).

This digital practice with entanglement and its potential for defining a future memory of you might point to the emergence of a privacy-savvy, publicly attuned Generation Alpha. But familiarity is not the same as understanding. Or at least Generation A has not experienced the historical shift from tech and media as something external, punctual, and to be called upon to aid and augment cognition and memory, to today's continuous connectivity, feed, or stream between head and wild. There are no buffers, no time out, in the making of memory on-the-fly.

Bartlett (1932, above) drew on the work of the neurologist Head (1920) and claimed that the process of remembering in the head involves the introduction of the past into the present to produce a 'reactivated' site of consciousness. From Bartlett's (1932) perspective, it is not a question of the past itself as an entity as such, but, 'our attitude towards' it and our 'organisation' of past experiences. Similarly, as Connerton (1989, 6) puts it: 'in all modes of experience we always base our particular experiences on a prior context in order to ensure that they are intelligible at all; that prior to any single experience, our mind is already predisposed with a framework of outlines .... The world of the percipient, defined in terms of temporal experience, is an organised body of expectations based on recollection'. But has Generation Alpha ever experienced or enacted memory in this way, *without* the on-the-fly pull of continuous digital connectivity and algorithmically driven 'predispositions'? And, in the restlessness of the memory feed, does anything ever stay still or stick around, so that we can point to it and say, '*this* is what I remember'?

At the same time, the memory feed is not so ephemeral as it may seem, not just in the unremembered self (above) of you, infinitely scattered, repurposed, and remembered across unknowable as well as knowable networks and archives, but in any individual's diminishing capacity to erase and forget unwanted experiences, events, and others, to *reset* the memory of them.

This, of course, is difficult when the details of our relationships, including how we have perceived them at the time—were they soft- or hard-launched? Why *did* you wait so long to hard-launch your relationship with this person? Were you having doubts?—is a matter of public record. Our ability to engage with a remembered self, that of who we were during a specific period or relationship, is affected by the fact that (1) our social media profiles are an unforgiving archive, unless we carefully attempt to edit and erase from them, an act of deliberation rather than a natural process, and (2) given the role that social media plays in how we communicate our feelings about relationships, the very arena within which memories are made is one that is shaped by its own conditions of overexposure. Your relationship is not happening unless it is happening online, but if it is happening online, its enduring memory will be the one captured by the rules of the virtual realm. This might not correspond with how you do or would have remembered the relationship on your own human terms or the terms of the people close to you in real life.

Perhaps then self-paparazzization (Merrin & Hoskins, 2025) wins the day, with the ultimate triumph of new memories that are incredibly individualised and, in a sense, deep, yet not necessarily coherent. Certainly, the memory feed upsets the two key traditional means of forgetting—of experience not being encoded into media/memory in the first place and the ultimate decay or failure of that media charged with holding memory. In Chapter 6, we explore this media and its relationship to us to identify the extent to which it is responsible for memory that, in the new digital memory ecology, is consciously and unconsciously outsourced to it.

6

Outsourced Memory, Outsourced Responsibility

The true cost of digital memory storage

The impact of storage on the actual condition of the memory itself is crucial. With the digital platforms available to us, storing memories in the form of photos or notes in ways that are convenient, for example, on the virtual cloud, is an attractive notion. However, such storage, offloading, or outsourcing memory may lead to the human brain being less likely to exercise the mnemonic activities known to increase the likelihood of future retrieval of such a memory from the internal source (brain), rather than the external source (Risko 2019).

Soares and Storm (2018), for instance, note that such a transactive memory system relies on 'prosthetic memory' devices such as a notepad, computer, smartphone, or the internet. While this may be beneficial in the short term because it allows individuals to focus on different tasks they may prioritise, it also means that our encoding processes of memories decrease and are likely to make more mistakes of encoding in the future. In this chapter, we consider further claims as to how digital and virtual storage, and more broadly cognitive offloading or outsourcing, shapes individual human memory in the head.

It is particularly important to consider this relationship if memory is seen as a digital creation. Henkel found that photographed objects are less well-remembered than observed objects (known as the photo-taking-impairment effect) (Henkel 2014). Similarly, Barnier's research into memory recall, which suggests, through a dog barking metaphor, that one does not have to bark if one has a dog; in other words, if something in our environment can substitute *us* in a particular venture,

The AI Memory Machine. Andrew Hoskins, Kristína Čimová, and Danny Pilkington,
Oxford University Press.
DOI: 10.1093/oso/9780198995906.003.0006

there is no need to expend personal energy on this task (Barnier 2012). Repeating such an exercise can, according to some, reflect in the brain's architecture over a long time period (Marsh and Rajaram 2019) and, by extension, it can also affect what is deemed to be valuable enough to remember for the future. Such thinking on a subjective and individual level can, logically, impact what is remembered of the present by future generations due to the value ascribed. Storage of convenience, rather than of prioritising, has been evidenced in what has been dubbed the 'Google effect' (Sparrow, Liu & Wegner 2011, Fawns 2022, Risko et al. 2024, Storm, Bittner & Yamashiro 2024).

As we have set out, the fragility of human memory has long been revealed by attempts to bring it external aid. However, shifting cultures and uses of technologies and media to document our world are also said to diminish our experience of it. For example, in a 1975 essay, the novelist Walker Percy describes a man who arranges a tour of the Grand Canyon. Yet, the man's *experience* is obliterated by his 40 years' worth of seeing and hearing about it. So instead of confronting the experience anew, he photographs it.

> Seeing the canyon is made even more difficult by what the sightseer does when the moment arrives, when sovereign knower confronts the thing to be known. Instead of looking at it, he photographs it. There is no confrontation at all. At the end of forty years of preformulation and with the Grand Canyon yawning at his feet, what does he do? He waives his right of seeing and knowing and records symbols for the next forty years. For him there is no present; there is only the past of what has been formulated and seen and the future of what has been formulated and not seen. The present is surrendered to the past and the future. (Percy 1975/2000, 47–48)

The camera here is used as a lens, which covers rather than illuminates that which it is pointed at. The urge to capture and keep the experience in the form of the photograph seems to override and undermine the actual experience itself. This is a nod to the significance afforded to the externalised future of memory of what might remain of an encounter if it is left only to the vagaries of the recollections of the human mind.

The diminishing value of the present does not just impact our experience of the present but our ability to remember in the future. As Resnick (2018) says, 'if we're not paying attention—if we're not even getting information into our short-term memories—nothing will be stored long term in our brains .... When we're hunting for the perfect Instagram shot, we're not listening, we're not smelling, we're not always paying attention to the beautiful, complex minutiae that make up the moment'.

But since Percy's writing, the external memory field has been utterly revolutionised with developments in social and digital media, and in generative AI. The connective turn across the early 2000s, the abundance, pervasiveness, and immediacy of digital media, communication networks, and archives, has forced a view unprecedented in history. This turn drives an ontological shift in what memory is and what memory does, paradoxically both arresting and unmooring the past. It has re-engineered memory, liberating it from the traditional bounds of the spatial archive, the organisation, the institution, and distributed it on a continuous basis via connectivity across minds, bodies, and personal and public lives. This opening up of new ways of finding, sorting, sifting, using, seeing, losing, and abusing the past, both imprisons and liberates active (intentional, conscious, purposive) human remembering and forgetting (Hoskins 2017, 1).

It is therefore unsurprising that following the connective turn, there has been a significant acceleration in psychological and experimental work devoted to testing the influence of different media forms and technologies, including internet usage, on the capacity and reliability of human memory (Marsh and Rajaram 2019, Henkel 2014). Furthermore, Schacter (2021) provides an excellent review of the impact of media and technology on four of his 'sins' of memory, developed from his influential *Seven Sins of Memory* (2001) notably seven categories of error or distortion of individual human remembering.

Yet, the twenty-first century has seen further and deeper digital transformations of living that have radically changed what memory is and what memory does. As outlined above, our work is not only motivated by tech revolutions' enhancing and diminishing of human memory but also seeks to illuminate how they shape owner, designer, and algorithmic imaginaries of what should constitute memory in the twenty-first century, and how it can remain a profitable commodity. This is a multi-directional relationship. Changes in technology affect what of the past can be aggregated, archived, shared, deleted, obscured, spliced, managed, and so on. Furthermore, the mass overproduction of the individual and entire societies in the digital age (more of this in a moment) creates a problem of volume and complexity that *appears* to require a technological solution. But in this very process, technologists and designers reimagine how human memory can be captured, seen, stored, used, shared, into something unrecognisable as 'memory' only 20 years ago. The race to solve the problem of the memory feed, in turn, drives the perpetuation of the memory feed.

Technological solutions to technological problems

The utility of a total memory has long been promised. In the early 2010s, following on from the initial researcher exclusivity of Microsoft's 'SenseCam', the promise of forthcoming 'lifelogging' devices began to stir up interest in the consumer market. The lifelogging device, *Narrative*, for example, promised not only photographic memory retrieval but also *organisation*. 'Relive your life like you remember it', its marketing video pronounced (Memoto 2013). This is *Narrative*: a GPS digital camera with tiny dimensions that you clip on to automatically take photos wherever you go.

The developers at *Narrative* therefore claim that it is useful because it captures the moments that we did not realise were moments until afterwards. In other words, moments that seem mundane and inconsequential, with the benefit of artificially produced hindsight, are actually moments we wished we had captured, to re-wind, re-live, and remember. Although the company announced its voluntary dissolution in 2016, having failed to secure enough backing and customers to be viable, the cheapness, portability, and pervasiveness of digital devices have increased so-called self-tracking and fast-developing technologies for mining supposedly useful data from daily life.

These imaginaries of memory have been more than realised, not through some wearable lifelogging device, but through the smartphone, expected to reach seven billion active smartphone subscriptions globally in 2026 (Statista 2025b). It is difficult to overstate not just how transformative the smartphone is of human memory, but how it is also collapsing as well as colliding the remembering and forgetting functions and capacities between the head and the wild.

The smartphone enables the personal recording, sharing, and archiving of the minutiae of our lives, experiences, movements, and thoughts, in the present. The memory feed is both personalised and individual, and yet crowd-sourced, on-the-fly, bringing the present into a new relationship with the past. Contemporary experiences are made real through their digital capture and churn. The very function of photography surely was to mark a moment, an experience, or an event as worthy of capture, of cherishing for future recollection. But today, the memory feed delivers constant connectivity with little time for pause to review or make sense of the accumulating archive of the self (without, that is, some support from a memory aid (app)).

Furthermore, the goal of recording and sharing today is to have the present validated by others. And it is impossible for us to grasp or predict how the newly generated overproduction of the self and experience might be accessible or usable in a meaningful way down the line. Constant connectivity does not just enable an occasional or punctual offloading of cognitive work of remembering onto digital devices, networks, and archives, but rather it shapes a more on-the-fly dependency, a kind of streaming of the self.

Memory through multisensory (virtual) experience

For Generation F, there has been a marked shift towards using short-video streaming platforms such as TikTok for news, updates, and crucially, as a way of recording life's experiences. A GWI report points to the rapidly increasing importance of digital visual communication for Generation Z, including being able to identify with others (Feeley, n.d.). Such a shift towards dependency on the visual and the complete transformation of communication and remembering is bound to change our general outlook on reality and the shape of our memories, in what Schacter

(2021) labels as the 'domain general'. In a 2021 interview with Hoskins, Schacter says that while there is no evidence indicating that the 'underlying experience of memory in multiple domains' is being altered by social media experience, it is not inconceivable that this could eventually happen.[1]

Consider the interface of apps such as Snapchat or TikTok, but also the proliferation of memes and GIFs in everyday communication. The effectiveness of such tools lies in their ability to communicate something in a split second, as part of a continuous flow of connectivity with/through content, rather than requiring the brain to do the heavy-lifting of visualising an idea based on its description.

It is as if all the metaphorical 'books' of our lives and minds are incessantly and inevitably being transformed into film or TV series versions of their more profound content, relying on a quick and inaccurate synopsis found on websites that profit from providing cheat sheets and quick fixes.

In this manner, the complex and painful emotion of a heartbreak or loss that would have been previously captured in an often-therapeutic manner of a journal, letter, or a single photograph to be passed down by generations, is reduced to a GIF of the latest TV series sweetheart crying in the middle of Central Park being sent over Facebook Messenger to friends and whoever else is out there in the connected world.

The professionals from the field of memory app design we spoke to on this subject emphasised this emotional exploitation of memory apps as one of their greatest strengths, enabling them to manipulate the user and their behaviour. 'Memories' today have been effectively incorporated into the dopamine hit industry geared towards the immediate superficial rush of approval through likes, comments, and shares.

The forging, processing, and prompting of memories is thus part of a system that rewards an ever-greater immersion in and dependency on algorithmically informed nudges. The spread, support, and survival of individual human memories, in other words, their collective or social existence, in the wild, has long been seen to be dependent on their validation or direction through the consensus (or manipulation) of others, groups, and institutions. As the founder of the modern study of collective memory, Maurice Halbwachs (1980, 23) asks, 'Don't we believe that we relive the past more fully because we no longer represent it alone, because we see it now as we saw it then, but through the eyes of another as well?'

It is digital nudging that then supremely combines the effects of the two elements to Halbwachs' formulation here of what is needed to forge trust or belief in memory. Even putting aside the forms of digital validation of an experience or event that come from its posting or sharing online, the visual memory nudge on your smartphone affords a veracity that suggests 'we see it now as we saw it then'. But memory apps and services such as *Timehop*, in fact, transform the contemporary experience of remembering things 'involuntarily'.

Voluntary memory is a process of actively working on one's own memories in order to consciously remember something good or to suppress more difficult experiences. In contrast, 'involuntary' memory is that which intervenes suddenly and unexpectedly in our consciousness, a kind of disruption of the present. This is often associated with some kind of reminder of a past experience brought back through a sensation such as a taste or smell. It is an idea famously associated with the work of Marcel Proust. Proust (1950/1912, 189) writes,

> ... when an odour, a taste, rediscovered under entirely different circumstances evoke for us, in spite of ourselves, the past, we sense how different is this past from the one we thought we remembered and which our voluntary memory was painting like a bad painter using false colours ... [He] will suddenly rediscover forgotten years, gardens, people in the taste of a sip of tea in which he found a piece of *madeleine* ... because they are involuntary, because they take shape of their own accord, inspired by the resemblance to an identical minute, they alone have a stamp of authenticity ... as they make us savour the same situation under wholly different circumstances, they free from all context, they give us the extra-temporal essence.

Artificial, sensory-memory making is becoming more common. The *Glasgow Herald* reports that at Glasgow's Tall Ship museum, the forthcoming AromaPrime feature will allow visitors to connect with and imagine the past by choosing from a selection of artificially produced sensations of the past (Williams 2024). For a sensory evocation of our personal memories, it is memory apps such as *Timehop*, which afford precisely this 'extra-temporal essence' not through an instant evocation of an experience *in real life*, but rather through the flash of an image on our smartphone.

Spontaneity and authenticity have become nudges, which are paradoxically produced, by the machine, and through all our former interactions with the machine. Proust (above) suggests the process of involuntary memory is also special given its capacity to revisit a past that has also been forgotten. *Timehop* and other memory apps that function in this way restructure the capacity of the individual to remember, in this particularly vivid way—through the shock of the old—but at the same time inhibit that which would ultimately have been forgotten.

(Social) media literacy

As we have considered, psychologists such as Schacter (2021) rightly caution as to the availability of evidence that social and digital media fundamentally transform the underlying experience of memory in wider society (at a 'domain general' level). But the overnight explosion in billions of individuals suddenly but routinely accessing entirely new pasts, through being confronted with a churn of involuntarily or at least algorithmically presented image memories, surely is on a scale that is doing precisely that.

But what are the prospects for resisting being carried away by emotional triggers in the dopamine-induced past? Often, the idea of battling digital modes of attention and of course memory capture are associated with a generational stage, a mode of knowing, and a process of remembering that comes from living through pre-digital existence. However, when it comes to emotionally triggered involuntary memories, the experts we spoke with tended to agree that there was no clear age gradient to levels of susceptibility.

If we accept this premise, however, we must necessarily accept that this type of credulousness affects our ability to absorb information, to process facts, let those facts shape our reality, and, ultimately, record that reality in an unreliable, digital manner. Where traditional notions of literacy provided one with the tools to understand information and critically interpret facts, today's idea of literacy is inseparably bound with not just the media but the digital media and the precarious post-trust or post-truth environment that is its natural habitat.

This threat of losing the very stuff of personality, humanity, and the ability to rely on identifying facts has been explored in popular culture. In the dystopian novel *Fahrenheit 451*, Bradbury shows us a reality already identifiable in 1953 where being consumed by screens with digital images creates a dependency and lack of capacity for critical thinking; this scenario is not that far removed from our own experience of today (Bradbury 1953). Without the availability of the analogue way of learning and remembering, we are bound to create a whole new *homo digitus*. The born-digital generation, therefore, has in equal parts a huge advantage and a disadvantage over the older generations, all cognisant of analogue remembering.

Technical proficiency with navigating the emergent media of this century is associated with the young. This is especially acute today at a time of transformational change of modes of communication whose very success is driven by their take up by billions of people predominantly under 30, a reversal of the generational hierarchy of older ownership, control, and use of many of the twentieth century's media and communicational forms. But technical proficiency does not necessarily equate to a capacity to grasp the potential for digital living to haunt at the future.

Whereas the traditional modes of the individual and familial, but also often patriarchal selection and curation of photographs, slides or home movies, offered a highly gendered vision of the past, such records were mostly limited or contained in their capacity to be seen and used. The smartphone may be seen to have vitally opened up the potential of the past to be more inclusive in affording any individual the unlimited capacity to record, share, keep, or delete whatever they deem appropriate of their minute-by-minute experience. However, the overproduced self and the overproduced past immediately beg the question: what of this astonishing scale of user-generated and user-shared digital documenting of the day will survive? Who will own, control, have access to today's astonishing and proliferating glut and on what basis will the past's curation and its meaning be decided? At the moment, this is very much in the hands of Big Tech, investors, and funders, those with a material interest in the datafication of society.

Yet, the acceleration of emergence between the recording or documentation of an event and its later wider revelation and dissemination, both unsettles and short-circuits contemporary memory, as though the digital present has annexed a post-scarcity past. This has profound consequences for anyone or any organisation, institution, or government wishing to keep secrets. Because the individual smartphone recording of the everyday became so rapidly routine, there at least followed a period of naivety or ignorance, as to the resulting record's potential to be shared and used by others.

Even former Prime Minister of the UK, Boris Johnson and his Chancellor failed to comprehend that their (and many others) being recorded by Downing Street staff socialising at the height of the COVID-19 global pandemic, in breach of the lockdown rules that they created and required the country to follow, would offer rich material for a scandal that became dubbed 'Partygate'.[2] Did they not think that such images, eventually plastered across the internet, the subject of a police investigation and a civil service inquiry, were likely to be made public, or were they confused as to what they had the potential to show? Either way, the scandal highlighted the challenges for grasping some of the key vulnerabilities of digital living and organisation and the limited potential there seems for their avoidance.

Perhaps the answer to the conundrum of why knowledge of the consequences of constantly recording and of being recorded does not translate into any kind of meaningful resistance is to ask a different question. That is to consider, what is the function of the digital overproduction of the self? It is through sending our reality out into the world that makes it real to us.

There are several intersecting challenges then for the individual, caught up in the desire to snap and to share, but also in attempting to find meaning in the infinite digital archive of experience.

The apps that make memory real and important

One memory platform that does appear to navigate some of these challenges is *1 Second Everyday*. According to the company's CEO, its central premise is to consider how value can be attached to the stream of the infinite archive that we produce, through rendering it accessible as well as shareable. The algorithmic imperative is to nudge the sharing of the dramatic, the extreme, and the attractive. However, that leaves behind huge memory holes of all that is not made for Instagram, all of the mundane moments that slip beneath the sheen of the extraordinary and yet which comprise much of our existence. In addition, difficult or traumatic experiences can also easily be elided from the digital record, and ultimately sometimes not encoded into memory.

Although the idea of capturing a more visual record of the everyday continuity of individual experience is not new, the digital self is routinely and continuously produced and shared, without seeming exceptional. The app *1 Second Everyday* offers a unique capacity to effortlessly reduce an extended period of existence into a flickering compilation of seconds. The difficult or traumatic moments are not erased or blocked or forgotten, but rather flattened in their contextualisation, within the parameters of the passing of a whole month, or months, viewed as a coherent and complete unit of time.

In their routine capturing and sampling of literally every day, apps such as *1 Second Everyday* potentially offer a less sanitised as well as less glossy version of the past. Even in the context of an era in which so much is routinely and pervasively recorded, memory apps and services still enable the capture and management of experiences that would otherwise have gone unrecorded and thus be inaccessible. This is contradictory to the position of *Narrative* (above) whose promotional claim was that it is useful because it captures the moments that we did not realise were moments until afterwards.

But of course, the personal meaning of events changes with time, as does our capacity and need to remember them. This also includes their meaning for others. For example, Cesar Kuriyama here reflects on one of his own *1 Second Everyday* videos, where he includes a hospital visit to a seriously ill relative, and his discussion of this decision with his sister-in-law in light of an upcoming TED talk in which he considered showing it to a wider public audience:

> I asked my sister-in-law, one of my last seconds of my first video is me in the hospital showing her the video. I said, "Hey, I'm giving this thing, it's called a TED talk." She has no idea what it was. "I'm not going to show this if you don't want me to show it. I recorded it for me, but I'm giving this talk and therefore, it's totally your call. I don't know if I feel comfortable sharing this if you don't. I definitely don't figure I'm going to share this if you don't feel comfortable having this out there." She was super like, "No, no, no, no. This is the thing." She was grateful to see what happened... For her, it was just like weeks of a gap in her memory.[3]

Most of the headlines around memory apps concern the unwanted and intrusive algorithmic reminders of experiences, which have been deliberately pushed aside or deeper into human consciousness. However, difficult or traumatic experiences can usefully be worked through and take on new meaning through being replayed and re-examined in memory in future times. Such value may be unrecognisable in the present moment. The *1 Second Everyday* movie then can transform the personal but also the shared orientation to forgetting the past, and in doing so can enable the filling in of 'gaps' in memory, as was the case with Cesar Kuriyama's sister-in-law, above.

In sum, smartphone apps such as *1 Second Everyday* offer a new way of apprehending the personal past through the sampling of the everyday. They enable new means of remembering, managing, and even treasuring difficult memories, not as some kind of rupture or unique exception, but rather, as part of the continuity of autobiographical experience.

There are, therefore, avenues of memory offloading out there that try to respect the experiences of the user. However, in order to stay true to their principles, and to keep stewardship over the data and metadata of their users, such platforms cannot afford to be free of charge. It remains to be seen how many of us are ready or able to pay for the new management of memory, and how the contours of such transactional relationships could alter with time. In outsourcing our memories, we surely outsource part of our agency.

We pay for free apps with data

In contrast to *1 Second Everyday*, apps which haggle for our memories on a daily basis that appear free are often part of a Big Tech ecosystem that uses and sells our data in various and untransparent ways. The 'On This Day' feature of the Facebook app, or the Apple 'Memories' app, for example, collate our memories, and apply a selective algorithm to feed them to us in a drip fashion. One of our expert interviewees cautioned as to the perils of sharing memories on these platforms for personal but also professional purposes and how older generations have been largely spared, perhaps until relatively recently, the intense scrutiny that Generation F have been born into, 'What did I care when I was in college? Thank goodness there wasn't Facebook in college because I just did not care and I didn't understand'.

The paradoxical promise of digital memories across many of the apps, devices, and platforms that we have explored is that of the pursuit of the management, access, and control of total memory. The acceleration of technological consumption and desire is the basis for an emergent fetishisation of a memory that seems somehow complete and entirely under user control. The overproduction of the self, recording of everything, and the advent of the search engine seduces us to imagine that there is a supreme archive that is available for individual harnessing.

This pursuit of control over and perfection in memory ultimately requires forgetting: omission, deletion, suppression, obfuscation, and erasure. As we mentioned earlier, the Google Pixel phone is the digital device, which claims to help you to remember or forget. The 'Magic Eraser' has an array of possible uses, including: 'Remove a contemporary car from a photo meant to look like the 1950s; erase a child that photobombed your selfie; take out the branch that got in the way of your autumnal apple picking shot' (Willie 2021). But this software enables you to amend any of your digital photos, including those depicting relationships—and people—you now want to forget, 'so you can finally erase your ex from the archive, too' (Willie 2021).

This affordance of editing our personal archives seems appealing in our apparent capacity to manage total memory, but Big Tech remains firmly in control. It seems unlikely that many users read the terms and conditions they accept in gaining access to digital services and platforms. Yet, we accept them for reasons of convenience. We need and are accustomed to instant access to our digital, everyday services. Notwithstanding the fact that nobody has time to read and understand terms and conditions, to attempt to carve this out of our day at the expense of continued app usage would be disrupting our digital and virtual, and therefore our real, lives.

It is important to note that the control or lack thereof over our own data and memories (and their digital nudging) is tied to the capability of technology to track and exploit our emotional states, as expressed by one of our interviewees, Jonathan Wegener:

> "Can you believe this was a year ago? Can you believe how young we look? Can you believe we were this foolish?" That, for me, is the interesting part. The emotional reaction you have to the data. That's what really surprised us when we built the prototype. This email that literally just sends you the name of a restaurant where you were a year ago. It's a one word/two word phrase with the context that you were there a year ago. It opens this flood of emotions around that particular memory of that because you're visualising that restaurant.[4]

For another of our expert interviewees, Matt Raoul, the potential for a totally remembered past to trigger a negative emotional response is, in a sense, something that empowers the user:

> But we know some memories aren't happy, and we decided we are going to give people control over their experience because they are the ones who are going to decide whether looking back at a painful memory is too painful for them right now .... Those things change, right? The power of a memory changes over time .... Our approach has always been a bit of you take the good and the bad, and we're not the

> best decision makers to decide which is which. We put it all out there, and if someone needs to close the app and take care of themselves, we know this. And sometimes, it's helpful to be reminded of how far you've come.[5]

The algorithm then is not to blame! The transition of responsibility is unequivocally here to the user and to their capacity to close the app, move on, and forget.

The basis of our technological dependency

It is no wonder that this cycle of suggested content, connected with convenience of offloading memories and information, along with the carefully timed and calculated nudges of apps and push notifications, has led to a technological dependency we can scarcely hope to be able to shake in the future. It is hard to pinpoint where exactly the tipping point of no return was, but we are well past it now. The dependency we speak of is also constantly propagated by companies seeking to create entire ecosystems around a device, operating system, app, or services. Snapchat, for instance, popular particularly amongst Generation Z and A is a good example, explained here in our interview with Jonathan Wegener,

> From my perspective, Snap is really reinventing the entire phone. They have video calling in there. Obviously, there is messaging at the core. There's now a camera roll feature, which is what memories is. There's games. There's television in there, Snapchat Discover. There's a map feature. There is a Find my Friends. There's 20 companies in one. Snap is very much following the play book of an Asian messaging company where they are, a million micro apps into one mega app.[6]

Convenience and pervasiveness attracts billions of new users to a platform or service, as with the rapid growth of Snap and other image- and short-video-based apps such as TikTok. Again, we can think of tipping points to consider the moment at which a platform or service seems utterly indispensable for making and maintaining relationships, for work, and for access to everyday services. As Ryan Calo, in one of our interviews, explains:

> The problem Collingridge says is, the dilemma, is that by the time you figure out what technology is going to do, it's become deeply entrenched and people are invested. It becomes very difficult to shelve technology at that point because it's become a part of public expectations.[7]

The embeddedness of smartphones and their associated apps in the everyday, along with the digital flywheel effects, creates and sustains a dependency. Daniel Schacter (in an interview with Hoskins, above) conceded that 'there probably is a form of dependency'. On the other hand, he stated that:

> ... it's not clear to me that that dependency is primarily driven by memory related issues as opposed to need for approval, involvement in a social group, things like that. I would imagine [these] really are the critical drivers of the dependency rather than something specifically related to memory.[8]

But today the idea of an active, willed, functional, deliberating human memory as fundamentally part of human identity, that healthily changes with time, is surely threatened in the face of the scale of the shape and content of the past being determined by digital nudges. Memory in the wild, then, has seized memory in the head.

Yet there remains a stubborn belief that there is scope for some kind of escape, some kind of wresting back control, beyond the much-promoted yet always-temporary idea of digital detox (a term that in itself acknowledges that this is an addiction):

> Yes, all the personal tech hygiene, I really want to believe it because I want to believe that we can each be a change agent and help design our own lives how we want. I wish I had more great things to say about it than hopes.[9]

This is something that is probably more akin to a popular belief that we have all experienced in some shape or form—a mind over matter argument. If only we can distance ourselves and stay really strong with cast-iron willpower, we can remove ourselves from technology and the modern world.

Szakolczai's (above) 'exiting the captaverse' ethnography is illustrative here, and we have seen this idea explored in popular culture too, for example the Viggo Mortensen film, *Captain Fantastic* (IMDb 2016) concerns an anti-capitalist father determined to educate and raise his children outside of the rotten structures, institutions, and technological advantages of the modern world. With the pervasiveness of the digital media ecology, and its structuring around neoliberal conditions that further compel engagement with it—on its own terms of individualism—this approach is difficult to apply. The dependency we speak of is not purely through personal addiction, it is because every aspect of our lives is subject to deep mediatisation, increasingly dependent on the ownership of a smartphone, for everything from travel, to banking, to home security, and to identification.

Within the context of memory, the dependency we speak of is a deeper type of dependency that stems from a commitment that is sold to us as a mere demo or a small step on the journey of offloading your memories, but which quickly takes over the entire enterprise of your ability to remember. Commitment to an app that will from now on take care of your photos and curate your memories is a commitment that cannot retrospectively be renounced.

This commitment implies a loss of ownership should we decide to move our photos elsewhere. It often implies financial commitment too, to whatever app is selected to keep our data. There is therefore an amount of trust we invest in apps and devices, stipulating an unwritten agreement that our photos and memories will be available to us indefinitely. But who is to say what happens to our memories deposited in these apps decades from now? What are the prospects that a given app (and its ownership) will survive to deliver on the continuous access to our personal photos that it promises?

On responsibility and accountability

> I think that one of the things that would matter to me is what kind of care is being taken in a curation of memories? Who is doing it for what reasons? (Ryan Calo)[10]

Who is accountable or responsible for the use of the memories—in terms of the digital acts we consciously and unconsciously commit to archive—in the future?

One of our interviewees, Jacob Appel, an expert in algorithmic analysis of websites and their use of data for target advertising, offered a more pessimistic vision beyond the mere nuisance of ads that seem to follow us around the internet:

> The use of other information about me and making decisions regarding me, like, can I get this credit card? Or do I get to take a student loan? Or things like that. Yes, I'm rather pessimistic about the possibility of really shielding the other information about me from the decision makers in those cases .... I do think we got here because companies, particularly just Google, Facebook, a number of companies offered products seemingly for free that were not actually free.[11]

If experts embedded in the field offer caution as to the limits of personal data protection, then most of us with only a lay understanding of the workings of algorithms, the means through which personal data is collected and the uses to which it is put, have little prospect of arresting such vulnerabilities. And this is an ongoing conundrum that continues to bewilder—if we at least suspect that personal information and media content about us, photographs, video, messages, and data of us, friends, travel, habits, sexuality, relationships, opinions, and memory are fundamentally compromised, being scattered and hackable in the wild—then why don't we do something about it?

The transformations ushered in by digital and imaging technologies have enabled psychologists and neuropsychologists to make huge leaps in our understanding of the nature and function of cognition and memory.[12] However, while technologies have helped bring memory in the head increasingly into the light, these have also pushed memory, its workings and influences, increasingly out of view and beyond human comprehension. In fact, there seems a close relationship between technological effect and human incomprehensibility; the more AI and algorithms determine what of our past is storable, findable, and shareable, the less we seem to know about how this happens. Without insight and control over such processes, we are losing our capacity to hold and manage memories and to render them both intelligible and usable.

As with any psychological experiment, what is knowable is ultimately reliant on the nature, reliability and quantity of data that is available, to be able to make claims about memory in the head or wild. Digital technologies and algorithms render the making and remaking of memory opaque to users. However, at the same time, user engagement with social media, apps, and platforms has produced an incredible new resource of data for exploring, developing, and manipulating today's highly datafied personal memory.

The technologists of memory, the creators, designers, developers, and owners of platforms more widely, but also specifically apps made to create and manage memories, possess incredible power and responsibility. This is in the form of their access to, gathering, use and application of personal data, including on user behaviour, in nudging, shaping, and reconfiguring what human memory is and how it comes to be made, remade, and used. That this, at a scale and often at a level of impenetrable complexity, affords memory technologists an incredible influence and status in the digital era.

There is a new war on memory with digital platforms and algorithms wielding power without accountability, in their supreme capacity to determine what is searchable, censored, or erased.

Jonathan Wegener, the app designer and original cofounder of *Timehop*, offers a clear sense of how the growth in collection of data connects with rendering such services viable and in transforming how memories can be accessed and used in new ways:

> The technical problem ends up changing over time in some interesting ways. When we started the service, when we started Foursquare seven years ago, I think 60% of the people that signed up didn't have

> a memory that day a year ago. Let's say we had 100 users; we were only sending 40 emails. We didn't have enough data to give people. We didn't have enough memories; we didn't have enough access to the past. Over the last 10 years that's totally changed. iCloud photos weren't a thing. All the iPhone photos were just looking on the camera roll. Most of those, I think 90% when we ran the numbers early on, of the users didn't have photos older than a year ago. We were really quite limited in the number of memories we could get access to.
>
> But now, with iCloud storage, with 10 years of digital postings, the problem has shifted to how do you filter and showcase the best ones and to de-duplicate them? Cut the noise and show the signal. Tie the signal and the noise. Yes, I've always found that interesting. Yes, anyway, so I don't think it's going anywhere. It's the habit of seeing what you did a year ago, but also just the different ways of accessing your memories. Whether it's cutting by location, calendar date, face search. There are many orthogonal ways of accessing those memories. It's pretty cool.[13]

This is the digital flywheel effect in action. The transformational shift to the routine uploading and sharing of, and by, the overproduced self, of messages, photos, and videos, offers a relentless accumulation of 'memories' to a tipping point at which there is a dependency on digital apps and services for the making, holding, and management of those same memories. This is the ultimate realisation of the memory feed in which to function in the digital tsunami, the remembered self has to collude with the technology: we give you more, so you need us more.

So, in terms of the challenge posed by Schacter (2021), outlined above, as to the digital effects on the memory processing architecture to the extent that these would alter the underlying experience of memory in the first place, we argue that we are already there. For us, this 'architecture' is the memory feed—how we give up or 'feed' services and platforms, organisations, and governments, and in this case, the new industry of memory, with our personal data and media content. And the digital flywheel effect is the enabling of the industry to nudge and feed us versions and visions of our overproduced selves and thus determine what is possible and impossible in memory in the future.

Jacob Appel, an auditor of algorithmic practices and a former algorithm designer, offered a useful perspective on the potential salience of this kind of digital nudging:

> Roughly speaking, in behavioural science when we say something is salient it means it's like at the top of your mind. It appears to you. The salient information in a picture is the information that pops up, that your eye is drawn to. What is salient in our memories is really important .... I believe that salience is a real concept, and I think it really does influence our cognition, I think that when a memory from a year ago is supplied, that really means we'll think about it, and we may not have thought about it before or absent that intervention .... I think it has a very profound ability to shape what we're thinking about on a minute to minute, hour to hour and day to day basis.[14]

And as we have suggested, there is something of a paradox in the digital nudging of memories against the experience of the spontaneity and authenticity of something that may have been forgotten. But also, this, for Matt Raoul (former CEO of *Timehop*), changes user orientation to an understanding of their past and how it might be revisited and remembered:

> I do think that it has changed people's actions now in terms of what they document and how they treat what they're doing now, thinking about what it's going to be in a year, when they do or don't see it again.[15]

On responsibility, then, how will the memory of today look in 20 years' time, who will own it and be able to access it, and how usable will it be? The answer will be determined by the workings of the memory feed and its algorithmic conditioning between user and industry, both of whom operate under the constraints of the conditions of capitalism. And it is to a focus on these aspects of control that we now turn to consider further.

7

Political Memory and the Anti-autobiographical Future

Official narratives

We have argued that traditional forms of human remembering and forgetting are diminishing, as they are replaced with an omnipresent, deeply pervasive memory understood by algorithms and owned by Big Tech. The outsourcing of memory incurs a simultaneous outsourcing of responsibility for how memory is used. It has long been the case that memory is politicised, disputed, and reframed to serve present ends, and this has occurred on both individual and social levels. In this chapter, we focus on the human tendency to attempt to revise the past for the needs of the present, and the risks of outsourcing all capacity for revision to technologies that are beyond our control. The AI memory machine stands to distort our world—it is aided in doing so because of the distorted data we fuel it with.

It has long been the case that official narratives are constructed to serve present political needs. Indeed, historiography and even archaeology are understood to be a means by which groups can assert influence and authority over the dead and their memory (Coenen 2020). Anderson (1993, 5–7) provides the example of monument-making during the Philippine's revolution in the late 1800s. Poet and novelist Jose Rizal, executed by Spanish forces in 1896, was memorialised in a statue erected by the revolutionary government a year after his death. The statue, its engravings, and the state's narrative about Rizal encouraged people to view him as a hero and a martyr, worth tributing through one's own martyrdom amid a revolution very much still in progress at the time. Other statues were erected in a similar tone, with the official narrative

The AI Memory Machine. Andrew Hoskins, Kristína Čimová, and Danny Pilkington,
Oxford University Press. © Andrew Hoskins, Kristína Čimová, and Danny Pilkington (2026).
DOI: 10.1093/oso/9780198995906.003.0007

around Rizal based on his 'substitutability'. By contrast, pilgrims ('Rizalistas') donned in revolutionary colours paid tribute at his monument in order to memorialise him as the one, the only one, an 'irreplaceable and unserialised' god-like individual that they could never reincarnate in their own actions.

The statue, then, facilitates two very different memories of Rizal: the official state memory and the one held by Rizalistas. It is worth noting a further point in the memorialisation of Rizal, which surrounds colonial interpretations of his revolutionary writings. Translations into dominant colonial tongues have seen meanings skewed to fit dominant narratives, which sees Rizal alienated from his own memory, the agency he possessed while alive subsumed in alternate meaning (Anderson 1993, 18).

Anderson goes on to provide further examples, of British soldiers from the Great War buried in mass military graves in France, with state-determined headstones, a 'nationalisation' of the dead seeing thousands captured in a British state-controlled memorialisation, the families of the deceased unable to reclaim the bodies for personal burials with agency over their memories (Anderson 1993, 14). Mass graves, monuments, and memorials are built to create and perpetuate official narratives, where the real dead are 'serialised, replicated, sequestered, forgotten' (Anderson 1993, 15). In these official memories, the legacies of the dead are cultivated to legitimise continued ruling ideas and framings of events. The purpose of physical spaces for remembering the dead is to serve this end.

Similarly, language and education are crafted to ensure we remember and forget the right things about the dead. It is a pre-requisite that we remember—through constant reminding—certain details yet in the same moment forget problematic aspects of the memory. Anderson (2006, 201) is worth quoting in full here:

> English history textbooks offer the diverting spectacle of a great Founding Father whom every schoolchild is taught to call William the Conqueror. The same child is not informed that William spoke no English, indeed could not have done so, since the English language did not exist in his epoch; nor is he or she told 'Conqueror of

> what'. For the only intelligible modern answer would have to be 'Conqueror of the English,' which would turn the old Norman predator into a more successful precursor of Napoleon and Hitler. Hence 'the Conqueror' operates ... to remind one of something which it is immediately obligatory to forget.

Further examples include Mark Twain's (still) culturally heralded Jim and Huck characters, who in 1881 were 'the first indelible image of black and white as American "brothers" ... companionably adrift on the Mississippi', however, as Anderson points out, 'the setting is a remembered/forgotten antebellum in which the black is still a slave' (Anderson 2006, 203). It is often expected of the reader that this contextual aspect is forgotten, and the symbolic meaning is remembered.

A further example is the national framing of the 'Spanish' civil war. While the conflict is remembered with this title and its localised 'civil' or 'national' character, at the time of its inception, the conflict on the Iberian Peninsula was 'an arena in which global historical forces and causes were at stake', with General Franco's 'Valley of the Fallen' necropolis built and reserved for those who, 'in [the Franco regime's] eyes, had died in the global struggle against Bolshevism and atheism'. These global and political contours, identifying the Spanish civil war as a locus for wider struggle between communism and fascism, risk being forgotten in an official memory of the 'Spanish' civil war (Anderson 2006. 202). Each of Anderson's examples invites us to consider the Halbwachsian perspective, that memories are in large part 'products of the symbols and narratives available publicly' (Olick 1999, 335), and that these symbols and narratives over time exert great influence over what is not only remembered but also forgotten.

Resurrecting the dead

There has long been a popular curiosity with the prospect of using technology to transcend the boundaries between life and death. Twenty years before the release of David Cronenberg's *The Shrouds* (IMDb 2024), the comedy sketch show, *Chewin' the Fat* (IMDb 1999–2005) had a scene where a webcam was placed in a coffin in order that the family could remain in touch with their deceased relative. Two decades on, this is a curiosity that technologists appear to have satisfied. Indeed, it is one that they have captured. The human wish to have one last conversation with a deceased loved one has been capitalised upon and sold back to society.

There is a growing market for AI products that enable your loved ones to communicate with you, or an artificially remembered version of you, after you die. Deadbots emulate the personality, behaviour, voice, and/or appearance of persons already deceased, and/or they are made to emulate someone once they are dead. There are two principal forms of deadbots. The first, retrospective on how data and information about you are carefully and/or carelessly produced and scattered over the course of your life, is available to be found, connected, and used to feed generative AI transformer models, once you are no longer alive. The second, prospective form of deadbot, is in the training of an avatar or chatbot to simulate someone once they are dead (Hoskins 2024). The spread of both forms of deadbot add to the ethical challenges of the booming 'digital afterlife industry' (Öhman & Floridi 2018) including over the nature, extent, or absence of consent, of the individual being 'recreated'.

The *prospective* form of arrangement is under more pressing consideration at the end of the living memory—of a person or even a generation. For example, in Hiroshima and Nagasaki, museums and community organisations are actively considering the use of AI to extend the virtual presence of the *hibakusha* (atomic bomb survivors). At the same time, AI applies a retrospective force on the past that resurrects the dead through renderings of their voice and image (Hoskins 2024). Some parents who have lost their children in gun shootings in the United States have used an AI voice generator to deepfake their dead children's voices for use in automated telephone calls to lawmakers as part of a campaign to push for greater gun control (Stern 2024). Although this may sound like science fiction, it is the reality of generative AI that is being deployed to weaponise memory today. The name 'grief tech' (Bryce 2023) is increasingly being attached to the plethora of services increasingly devoted to the AI resurrection of your lost loved ones. These also have considerable consequences for the living, on mental health (Mulligan 2024), and on 'networked labor' (Kneese 2023).

Hans Block and Moritz Riesewieck's 2024 film, *Eternal You* is a prescient interrogation of the new market in which 'companies create avatars of deceased persons, so that their loved ones can interact with them' (Sundance Institute 2023). The film follows the experiences of some of grief tech's first users, asking important questions of whether the trajectory is a healthy one. The film directors believe that it is the developers of these products that are responsible for the outcome, not end users: 'you are responsible for your invention', says Riesewieck (Cine-Fix 2024). Yet, as well as holding the system of technological production to account, the film also highlights the enduring appeal of this technology for users: 'Artificial intelligence promises us what religion does, you don't have to die, you can be reborn someplace else in a different form' (Dogwoof 2024).

Here, AI is portrayed as a force that does not just replicate and even improve human behaviour, but rather it transcends it and provides a form of 'life' that the human mind and body cannot. The 'god-like' position of AI, with its towering and surveilling eye seeing everything we do, affords AI a perception of us that can amount to a new version, or form, of our 'self' entirely.

Riesewieck and Block (2022) argue that this is a transformation of the concept of the soul:

> Tech companies are making increasingly aggressive inroads into a territory that was for a long time the purview of our gods and lovers: the ability to truly know a human being, to recognise them.

In contrast, the soul is something that Big Tech are able to interpret as the 'us' we leave behind in our digital acts. The commodity value of this soul, and indeed the personal value of it to family members desperate to reconnect with a version of 'us' after the real us is gone, leaves technology companies in a significant position of power. But it is no wonder there is a market for products that ostensibly transcend the boundaries of life and death; this happens through datafication anyway. As Kneese (2023, 6) puts it,

> Data stick around, embedded in objects on people's bodies, like Fitbits and other wearable devices, and in smart office and home products like Amazon Echo, Ring, and Google Nest. The data of the dead and the living commingle. Such indecipherability leads to unease, maybe even horror, while stoking fantasies about living on beyond physiological death.

In a sense, then, our datafied self, the one we never really knew, lives on after we die regardless. Through grief tech, our families can form a relationship with some kind of combination of this algorithmically imagined self and a self that is based on our image and voice. But whether they decide or can afford to do this, as Kneese highlights, they and the rest of the world will forever share the ether with the datafied selves of all who have come before and since been lost.

The growing market for technological 'solutions' to the problem of death and being written, re-written, preserved and immortalised in history, despite the risks this poses for the wellbeing of the living, is another example of capitalism's insatiable drive for profit coming at the expense of positive social and human development.

Distorted starting point, distorted memory

The distortion of memory is a complex and common practice. Let us begin by offering a perspective on how memory has the capacity to build on basic recollections of events that have occurred. The influential psychologist and neuroscientist Endel Tulving poses that human memory is unique in its tendency to build on semantic memories (a storage of general facts) with episodic memories (personally experienced events) (Tulving 2002, Bendrat 2023).

For Tulving, 'episodic memory is oriented to the past in a way in which no other kind of memory, or memory system, is. It is the only memory system that allows people to consciously re-experience past experiences' (Tulving 2002, 6). In this sense, it is a form of time travel, whereby humans use their consciousness of subjective time—their *autonoesis*—to re-experience a past event, to be transported to a different reality—the reality of the mind—an activity quite different from dreaming or imagining the unknown (Tulving 2002, 2).

This human capacity for mental time travel is a level of awareness that 'allows autonoetic creatures [human beings] to reflect on, worry about, and make plans for their own and their progeny's future' (Tulving 2002. 20). In other words, human memory, and the layered semantic and episodic intelligence giving it shape, allows us to re-imagine the events of our lives with great subjectivity and, as such, uniquely (despite perhaps inaccurately) imagine our own futures. Alternative understandings to those of Tulving determine that episodic memory is less concerned with how we as individuals believe past events transpired, but rather, the manner in which we justify our beliefs about events (Mahr & Csibra 2018). Either way, it can be said that episodic memory is, in some sense, how we reconcile our perceived self with the things that we have done and which have been done to us in our lives.

Further theories understand episodic memory as *generative*, able to *construct* and *reconstruct* the moments of our lives, sometimes as part of a *scene construction* process that happens when we remember events (Dings & Newen 2021, 92). Dings and Newen apply a theory of 'scenario construction', wherein cues bring about the retrieval of memories and, in turn, the episodic 'gist' of what happened, as well as the relevant semantic information retained in memory. This framework sees that 'any constructed scenario may feed into subsequent instances of scenario construction by affecting the gist or semantic information' (Dings & Newen 2021, 92). It is worth noting that this facet of human memory is reminiscent of one of the primary concerns around AI: that it will generate and re-generate bias-laden falsehoods, based on previously regenerated falsehoods, leading to a post-truth scenario (Benson 2023, Bell 2023). The issue with AI, of course, is the scale and efficiency with which models can engage in this process.

Memories are a blend of fact and fiction. Anna Bendrat's (2023) study of episodic memory as presented within Jordan Harrison's play about AI, *Marjorie Prime*, shows us the potential for AI models to re-constitute our identities with episodic data. The play follows Marjorie, who suffers from dementia, and her family's disagreement over how much information about Marjorie's life to feed her AI companion (a hologram of her late husband). The issue is whether an AI with too much information, able to remind her too many details from her traumatic life, will cease to be supportive and in fact undermine the newfound liberty she is experiencing in her new present—a present that is *untethered to her past.*

As the story unfolds, it becomes clear that the AI is not necessarily functioning as intended: a tool to remind people of things that are fading from their memory. Instead, the AI is simply carrying and reproducing the episodic, therefore biased, memories being fed into it by human agents. Marjorie's memory of how she met her husband is fed back to her by the AI, presented as truth, yet in fact reflects an inaccurate and embellished rendering of the story told cunningly by Marjorie in an earlier scene. Thus, instead of providing an interactive glimpse into 'snapshots from family albums which can always be retrieved in the same form, rather, they [episodic memories recorded in AI] are malleable formations tinted with bias by attributing to them emotion or knowledge we acquired after the event' (Bendrat 2023, 221).

In Marjorie's case, it was she herself that changed the story of how she met her husband. Yet, with the AI empowered and designed to perpetuate the stories it has been fed, the true story, or at least its starting point, becomes lost. When we outsource our memories to AI, even if we play an active role in forming them at the point of outsource, the bias or distortion embedded in this formation is licenced as permanent; we might evolve, but the memory will be haunted by its earlier distortion.

The photograph capturing a moment in the past can be looked at and understood a thousand different ways by the same person looking at it from the perspective of their present, at a thousand different points in their life. A written story captures a moment that readers can understand and interpret differently as circumstances change; both the story and the person reading it, therefore, retain their agency, as the story remains as true as it was the day it was written, while the meaning can change for the reader every day they have read it since. The difference with Marjorie's story, outsourced to an AI that will perpetuate that which it is given, is that the original, 'true' story disappears altogether, and the meaning, the one implanted at the time of outsource, remains the same forever.

Bendrat's analysis of *Marjorie Prime* raises important questions of the future of AI, agency, and truth. We are prompted to recognise that an

AI will re-produce that which it is fed, so while not necessarily possessing the human capacity to episodically remember events (yet), AI is a tool by which humans can—consciously or subconsciously—have their episodic memories carried and memorialised. Our ability to travel in time, physically rooted in the present but worrying about the past and its implications for the future, encourages us to quell the real anxiety of the present with rationalisations and re-imaginings of past events and their consequences. Human storytelling involves embellishment and narrative-building, but whether we want to hand over these storytelling reigns to powerful AI models that can infinitely produce and re-produce information based on what we—and/or others—feed them, is another matter. Rather than the AI-induced prompts of the future producing an emergent, reconstructive past for the present, in Bartlett's terms (above), will all we be left with is memory that is entrapped by the limits and biases of the programmable past?

The *anti*-autobiographical future

The concepts fictionalised in *Marjorie Prime* are not far off current explorations in the field of dementia research. Researchers at the National Robotarium, a partnership between Heriot-Watt University and the University of Edinburgh, are developing an AI companion for people suffering with dementia.

> Agent-based Memory Prosthesis to Encourage Reminiscing (AMPER) will explore the potential for AI to help access an individual's personal memories residing in the still viable regions of the brain by creating natural, relatable stories. These will be tailored to their unique life experiences, age, social context and changing needs to encourage reminiscing (Healthcare in Europe 2022)

According to AMPER's grant application (UKRI 2021), 'the project will collect both generationally relevant and personally relevant multi-media materials organised and reorganised by the agent's autobiographical memory ... Autobiographical memory provides a reflection of "self" enabling an individual to relive an event'.

This poses questions of agency and episodic memory. Who will or could determine the 'generational' memory prompts, and how could their biases be carried and developed by the AI? The point here is not to cast aspersions on the value or use of the tool itself, but to consider the fundamental re-ordering of the memory-making and storytelling process when it is outsourced to AI that does not simply store memories for us to make meaning of but prompts us to ascribe certain meanings to memories, making the AI an active agent in the formation of memory.

Consider the app OttoStory, introduced in Chapter 3's focus on the memory feed. OttoStory is a digital autobiography service where users pay to 'meet Otto, your AI biographer, guiding you through a reflective journey of your life's experiences'. Otto's services are paywalled; however, OttoStory's unique selling point is that they 'help transform your cherished memories into a captivating memoir' in an accessible way: 'say goodbye to professional writers and high costs'. Herein lies one of AI's most heralded potential virtues: providing high-quality professional services at little cost, making services accessible to a wider range of people. While this potential holds genuine benefits, it perhaps paints an incomplete picture of the previously human service being replaced, and the reasons access to that service has been the historical preserve of wealthy people.

While human biographers carry their own (often profit-based) motives, they remain professional writers with a reputation of their own to uphold. Their relationship with the people they write about, dead or alive, comes out in the writing and we, readers, can analytically hold this relationship to account. An AI has no reputation to uphold. The company who built its model does, however, in the case of OttoStory, the very premise is that the AI simply helps you to write (dictate) your own story, in your own words, meaning the responsibility for how your story plays out is yours (OttoStory's website promotes very positive user reviews of accuracy). This is quite an empowering prospect, yet it poses challenges.

The final story, ostensibly *your* story, is a product of you, the AI, and the people who developed the AI, but this relationship and the disparate accountabilities within it are obscured. When you outsource your memory to AI, are you still responsible for it? The website promotes its 'emotion recognition' capabilities as follows: 'Engage with thought-provoking prompts crafted by psychologists, while Otto, sensitive to your emotional tone, ensures your storytelling remains authentic and deeply resonant'. This places a lot of trust on the ways in which these prompts—created by nameless and faceless psychologists—are positioned, and the types of emotion they are programmed to elicit, encourage, or enhance.

Furthermore, the agentic capacity of the human storyteller is challenged in that 'emotion recognition' built into the AI 'ensures your storytelling remains authentic and deeply resonant'. Here, it is suggested that AI plays an active role in *securing* the authenticity of human legacy. In other words, the AI picks up on our language, tone, and personality, to support us in saying what we *really* mean; to help us tell the story we *really* want to—according to the AI and its inputs. The AI provides users with questions, 'meticulously designed by experienced psychologists' to help you navigate the periods of your own life, 'ensuring meaningful and reflective storytelling'.

It is unlikely to be the case that OttoStory or its human designers intentionally intend to manipulate users and their stories, and the concept of AI dictation as a memoir-writing tool is no doubt valid and useful. However, the *active* role AI plays in 'ensuring authenticity' within such tools invokes old traditions of social memory construction processes that see individuals—especially those who are alienated from structural power—lose control of their own story. Historically, this has manifested in cases where empowered *living* storytellers speak on behalf of the dead. In his analysis of memorialising as a form of building national identity, Benedict Anderson refers to a 'self-appointed historian of the Revolution' in 1800s America:

> [He] not only claimed to speak on behalf of large numbers of anonymous dead people, but insisted, with poignant authority, that he could say what they 'really' meant and 'really' wanted, since they themselves 'did not understand'. From then on, the silence of the dead was no obstacle to the exhumation of their deepest desires. (Anderson 2006, 197–198)

The anonymous dead here cede not only their biographical output to a stranger but also their legacy, the lasting record of their intentions and wants. In the case of AI autobiography tools, it is the living who are at risk of making a similar concession, for their own memoir, their autobiographical record, has been crafted using a template provided by someone (or something) else—the same template used by many other users of the product whose experiences and emotions register the same predictive prompts from the AI model. The precedent set by OttoStory in the absence of regulation and sufficient debate on the purpose of autobiography, perhaps somewhat cynically leads us to fear an *anti-autobiographical future*: a future where we tell hyper-individualised versions of the same story, with emotion and insight registered in the same way due to our reliance on the same (malleable—yet not by us) template.

And it is this template that is vulnerable to being constructed and bound by ruling ideas, to serve elite interests. Furthermore, OttoStory pledges to 'immortalise' our stories in its format—but need they be captured as such? Is it necessarily positive that all of our stories, dictated to a device by us in a highly personal stream of consciousness (with AI 'prompts'), reach this level of complete record? While OttoStory 'guarantee complete security and confidentiality of [our] personal narratives and information', will fine-print loopholes, legislative change, and a lack of industry regulation mean similar models evade such promises in the future?

A further issue with the use of AI models to support autobiography is the human role in re-imagining one's past, present, and future. An autobiographical AI tool, offering a reflection of the user's own account of themselves, could perpetuate and develop an imagined self that, as was the case in *Marjorie Prime*, is a re-imagining of reality, a reconstruction of the past. It is not necessarily a bad thing that AI's have the power to store and replay our episodic memories, for there is nothing wrong with episodic memories. The issue is the extent to which the AI can distort these over time, redefining authenticity in the process. Our identities are in part a product of self-creation not only through a present-time experiencing of events but also through the narratives we create through memories (Dings & Newen 2021, 90).

Human memory, then, already revises the past to construct future-defining narratives. AI technology, a central component of the memory feed that shapes the memory of Generation F, is on a trajectory that will see this tendency proliferate, removing humans further from the truth—be this semantic or a person's own episodic interpretation, a form of truth in itself.

To elucidate the distinction between this human process and its version in AI, we return to the work of Anderson (2006, 204). He argues that the changes wrought by puberty make it 'impossible to "remember" the consciousness of childhood'. Instead, he says, there is 'a huge modern accumulation of documentary evidence (birth certificates, diaries, report cards, letters, medical records, and the like)', which reminds us how much we have forgotten yet how things have indeed fallen a traceable trajectory. 'Out of this estrangement comes a conception of personhood, *identity* ... which, because it can not be "remembered," must be narrated' (Anderson 2006, 204). While identity-building in this sense pre-dates AI, the 'documentary evidence' cited by Anderson here is but a fraction of the information recorded about our lives in the age of AI. With humans 'replaced' by AI in the process of narrative construction, there is a real risk that memories, legacies, and futures will be determined by an abstraction for which the humans of Generation F, including the humans closest to the those being remembered, have had little say.

In allowing us to re-experience events through mental time travel, episodic memories let us project our present selves onto past or indeed future events (Ding & Newen 2021, 89). This constructs an idea of these events, and how they might have unfolded, or will unfold, that is not necessarily a material reality. In turn, episodic memories, in a practical distortion of hindsight, allow us to encode past events with new meanings: 'the thing that happened, at the time felt like X, but with the benefit of what I know now or who I am now, I realise it was really Y, therefore I should do Z'. Thus, the memory of an event, and potentially the real-world recourse for this event as precipitated by how the event is (now) understood, become subjective historical revisions and distortions of the 'original' past.

Yet, in our digital memory ecology, how can we shape ourselves and our futures when our legacies are beyond our control? How can we learn and grow when memory, of self and of community, is not constructed socially, not contested between human agents, but which is abstracted through machinic processes? The digital memory ecology flattens out originality and agency. It leaves us stranded at sea, each scattered across fragments of rock that emerge from the swell at exactly the same angle, yet reside just far apart enough that we cannot hear each other speak over the roaring storm. In this period of shared solitude, the self is the ultimate refuge.

Learning from ourselves: the neoliberal loneliness crisis

In neoliberalism's disconnected and atomised society, it is easy to see how loneliness has become such a problem (Cantor 2024). Technology contributes towards the conditions for loneliness, where we feel removed from the prospect and merit of collective endeavour and social development. Yet, it also provides solutions. Popular AI companion apps (see also Chapter 3) such as Replika, Character.AI and Kindroid heralding the 'memorybot' era (Hoskins 2026), are seen to offer human-like emotional support and empathy. But what is lost is the social development that comes through conflict and collaboration with other humans.

Popular culture offers further insights on this direction of travel. In Spike Jonze's 2013 sci-fi film *Her* (IMDb 2013) the lonely and recently heartbroken protagonist Theodore Twombly finds new companionship, joy, and warmth in the blossoming relationship between him and his AI 'OS'—now being compared over a decade on with the very real ChatGPT-4o (Roose 2024)—whose female voice (chosen by Theodore during setup) acknowledges that 'her' knowledge is in great part influenced by interactions with Theodore. His habits and perspectives become embedded in 'her' self, and Theodore willingly retreats into this highly personalised virtual social reality. Eventually, drawing on data from beyond that which Theodore gives her, the AI develops an intelligence that transcends that of Theodore. His imprint on her, once focal, becomes a general, replicable, and numerable data input. Theodore is subsequently discarded, alienated from the meaning of his imprint on *her* and from his own sense of self.

Sierra Greer's 2024 novel *Annie Bot* (Greer 2024) charts a more sinister rendering of this kind of inward-looking dependency. Doug and his AI companion, Annie, are receiving relationship counselling because AI-Annie has had an infidelity with Doug's (human) best friend. The counsellor points out that Doug's increasingly alarming, violent, and possessive abuse of his 'bot' is an unhelpful and vengeful projection of his own problems of jealously and insecurity, and that given Annie is programmed to reflect behaviour, things may improve between them if he shows forgiveness. Inflicting patriarchy and misogyny on his companion proves not only an abusive but also an unhelpful and unsustainable means by which to develop his relationship and himself. Struggling with the idea, at one stage Doug suggests carrying out a 'reset' on Annie and restoring her memory to before the affair happened (it is worth noting that Doug says the complete memory would still be stored on a server somewhere after reset. He may be able to revise history in his own virtual world—but Big Tech will remember everything). Yet by wiping the affair from her history, he would not need to deal with the conflict it generates inside him by manifesting in their interactions as a problematic memory. Doug notes that he does not want Annie to be robotic, that he sees value in her being 'real', yet clearly, when this point is achieved by the AI and as a result Doug is forced to reflect, he instead suggests using the AI's capacity to help him forget.

The age of AI, with its infinite means of datafied remembering, also heralds a new era for forgetting. The idea of a reset, or partial reset, allows those in control of feeding and maintaining AI to cultivate its base of knowledge, learning, and predictive output. Rather than contending with history, observing its process and consciously, actively being a part of it, one could simply choose to revise it. This represents a retreat from opportunities to expand individual or social horizons, preferring instead the cosy and unchallenging terrain of an imagined, ideal self.

A retreat of this kind comes at a cost. On the level of the individual, our human development is stunted; our place in the contested and constantly moving process of history stagnates, in an attempt to cheat time. For communities and wider society, individualistic retreat comes at the expense of collective interest and control.

Colonial memory

Nigerian author, Chinua Achebe once said, 'It is the storyteller who makes us what we are, who creates history. The storyteller created the memory that the survivors must have—otherwise their surviving would have no meaning' (Bandele, in Achebe, 2001: X). First published in 1958, Achebe's *Things Fall Apart*, deals with this problem by centring the experiences, perspectives, and traditions of West African communities torn apart by European colonialism in the nineteenth and twentieth centuries.

We witness colonisers fragmenting society by sowing seeds of doubt, creating a division of interests, and perhaps most significantly, stripping culture, communities, and people of their dignity. Achebe's insights help us to understand colonialism's tactics of disempowerment. Towards the end of the *Things Fall Apart*, a community elder speaks to the younger generation about the strength that comes through unity. He suggests that when unified interest is fragmented and individuals pursue their own, new objectives instead, they do so not just at the expense of the community's culture and traditions but also of the collective power held by those who unite as one voice (Achebe 2001 (1958), 122).

Achebe's wisdom tells us a lot about where we are today, as a lesson on how the powerful create lines of division that have us all pointing fingers in different sideways directions, but never simultaneously upwards, and more specifically, how Big Tech drives and profits from an individualistic ideology that weakens our capacity to get together, as one, and ask questions. These may include: is it really worth forfeiting this level of personal data and control in order for an activity to be made slightly easier? In fact, has it even been made easier? Does this technological solution really just address a problem caused by technology in the first place? Who is benefitting from technology being used in this way? Who asked for this to happen and who decides what happens with it next? And hold on, if we do not have a say in this, how are we going to make sure it works in our interest, not the interest of the super-rich?

Why does the EU allow border agency Frontex, its most heavily funded asset with a 2020 budget of half a billion dollars, to take part in illegal and violent pushbacks and use racist bias-laden experimental AI technologies that lead to the torture and death of migrants? (Molnar, 2024b: 56–60, 62, 94–95).

To begin to grasp these questions, we turn to consider the democratic limitations of capitalism's techno-solutionism in practice.

If we accept the fact that on a material level, society is composed of two groups of people with broadly and fundamentally competing interests (shareholders versus low-waged employees, landlords versus tenants, colonisers versus the colonised), it becomes easier to understand the relationship, or tension, between techno-capitalism and democracy. Does techno-capitalism, as we have defined and described it in this book, enable global populations to exercise greater democratic will over the rules, powers, and conditions that influence their lives? Or, does techno-capitalism's pre-requisite forfeiture of personal data and its hyper-individualistic rendering of society leave us somewhat empowered as individual consumers but disempowered as citizens? We believe it is the latter.

Human rights lawyer and academic, Petra Molnar (2024b, 9) frames this problem as a 'tech divide', where there is a broadening gap 'between those who are able to design tech and those who are subject to it'. Some people make the decisions around technology—what it does, how it does it, when and where it is applied and for what purpose—others have these decisions inflicted upon them. These two groups of people have fundamentally opposed interests.

It should be of little surprise that these conflicts shape many aspects of life and often involve the same people. Shareholders have a stake in suppressed wages; workers have a stake in wage increases. Landlords have a stake in rent hikes, tenants have a stake in rent reductions. Colonisers have a stake in land and people brought under their control, the colonised have a stake in the restoration of their sovereignty. While issues can be and are complex (for example, where 'coalitions of interest' form on issues and passive consent blurs the lines between immediate and long-term interest (Gilbert & Williams 2022)), on a basic level, this is the reality of how material interests are divided in a system driven by their division. The 'tech divide' is just another arena where this tension plays out.

Eichhorn (2019, 14–16) breaks down forgetting, as it is experienced and used by migrants for survival. She highlights a distinction between the migrants and displaced of the twentieth-century post-war period and those of Europe's 2015/16 Syrian and North African refugee crisis. Migration in the digital, social media, and AI age is characterised in some ways by the construction of memory and its subsequent permanence.

The recent exponential growth in the complexity and volume of personal data and in metadata such as GPS location, device identifiers, and browsing and chatbot history, are resourcing ever deeper and wider, prediction, identification, and surveillance. For example, the US National Security Agency's SKYNET programme of mass surveillance of Pakistan's mobile phone network, collected metadata from 55 million users, and employed a machine learning algorithm to rate the likelihood of a given person being a terrorist. Thus, if your 'pattern of life' metadata corresponds with that of known terrorists, then you are identified as a target (Ford & Hoskins 2022). Furthermore, faced with the ongoing problem of even knowing who the enemy was in its war in Afghanistan, the US implemented a huge, digital biometrics programme capturing detailed biometric data 'on 80% of Afghanistan's 22m population' (Jacobsen 2021, 242).

In the case of Israel's genocidal campaign in Gaza and illegal occupation of Palestine, advanced AI technologies (*Lavender* and *Where's Daddy?*) are being used to identify targets and track the detail of their movements, in order that the Israeli military can then bomb them in their family homes (Abraham 2024, Downey 2025). The scale of such data sets and the ways in which they are minable and how individuals are identifiable, locatable, and trackable, demonstrate the potential of AI in manufacturing past, present, and future in support of political interests.

A past that is assembled from data reverses our right to be forgotten through traditional forms of memory decay, in that the more data that is collected about someone, the more they become vulnerable to identification and surveillance in the archives of the broken past. There is thus a reinforcing loop built into AI systems, as Kate Crawford explains, 'The machine learning approaches of Palantir and its ilk can lead to a feedback loop, where those included in a criminal justice database are more likely to be surveilled and thus more likely to have more information about them included, which justifies further police scrutiny' (2021, 198). This maximum data imperative also underpins the apps, services, and platforms that enable us to manage our own digital pasts. There is a collusion of technology with the remembered self, of convenience and control, of overload and sense-making; we give you more, so you need us more. Here the digital flywheel effect of a relentless accumulation of and learning about the datafied individual leads to a tipping point. This includes the reaching of an unstoppable momentum in the production and management of digital memories.

Migrants now rely on smartphones for finding out information about safe routes, translations, and how to be smuggled while avoiding the police. Médicins Sans Frontiéres, for example, use TikTok to share helpful information for people on the move (Molnar 2024b, 201–202). Then, when migrants arrive at their destination, smart phones are equally important for integrating into the new society while maintaining links with home (Koigi 2021). This connectivity is of such high value that migrants have been reported to prioritise it over clothing and healthcare, in some cases swapping food rations for airtime and data (UNHCR 2016).

Being connected also provides a means of telling your own story. This was the case for 19-year-old Rahaf Mohamed, who in 2019 fled her abusive family and used Twitter to share her experiences, which in turn amounted to a case for asylum granted by the Canadian government. The #SafeRahaf hashtag was used over half a million times within 24 hours of Mohamed's first tweet (Koigi 2021). Yet, Eichhorn (2019) draws a distinction between this publicly documented memory of trauma and the purposely forgotten trauma of post-war Holocaust survivors. For migrants in the age of social media, the age of Generation F, how will they ever be able to process memories in such a way that allows them to choose what they and others forget?

Disempowered memory

Eichhorn (2019, 22–24) roots this proposition in an analysis of the changing nature of childhood. In the past, childhood memories were in a sense constructed by adults; they came in the form of photo albums, yearbooks, and mementos. Maturing was a process of seeing these snapshots and revisions of the past and then moving on from them, remembering them as we wish to and forgetting as required and chosen. There is a power one has over their own memory that comes from being able to misremember, misrepresent, and forget. The permanence of social media curtails this power: 'If we were once able to edit or "overwrite" our childhood memories in order to carry forward only information deemed relevant or tolerable, we are now entering an era in which our relationship to the past is out of our control.' Unlike a yearbook or shoebox of memories, social media memory is interlinked and connected; our memories are shared and tagged and captioned as therefore distorted: 'traces of the past are now networked, linked, and never fully in our control.'

Anthropologist David Graeber (2018) analyses the impact of capitalism, in particular neoliberal capitalism, on the level of control we have over the work we do and the social and personal benefits we reap from it. Like Eichhorn, his proposition draws on a conceptualisation and construction of childhood and maturation. Under medieval feudal conditions, Graeber says, people would mature much later in life; in a social sense, this means marrying and owning a business. Up until the age of around 30, wealthy would-be suitors would frolic around until their family deemed them old and worthy enough to be bequeathed some land on which to make money. Rather than frolicking, poorer members of a community would spend this time working as an apprentice and saving up enough money (if male) or social capital (if female) to socially qualify as worthy of marriage, with the funds to run a business and employ the next generation of young apprentices. This social contract made quite clear the distinction between young people in transition and fully formed adults. The tipping point and dividing line centres around control and power. To be an adult, a fully formed and functioning member of society, is to have power over one's own destiny.

Graeber goes on to say that capitalism ruptured this contract and threw its rules, obligations, and social pathways into disarray. Where before there was a (more) genuine free market, with craftspeople running businesses on land rented from feudal lords, now the economic system produced monopolies. With big businesses and corporations in charge of production and in ownership of the means of production, more and more adults (defined by age) would spend their lives in receipt of a labour wage, owning and having a say over nothing themselves. This loss of agency reimagined what adulthood was, if it even existed, and effectively threw entire classes of people into a form of permanent childhood (by previous frameworks), an entire life lived not fully in control of one's own conditions, and therefore, not fully formed as an adult.

This assault on dignity and alienation from one's own place in past, present, and future, draws undoubtable comparisons with social media's capture of the self. Memory, and the social contract of maturation, development, and control that is bound by it, is under threat of a new set of rules, governed and controlled by Big Tech.

Children now share with adults the ability to produce and represent their experiences of their own accord through a digital production of the self (Eichhorn 2019, 11), a lot of which comes via selfies. It is hard to know what the impact of this overproduced, distorted, and never-forgotten self will have on Generation F.

The meaning of truth

While the lasting impact of the AI memory machine on Generation F is still to be seen, in this book, we have attempted to sketch out its parameters and risks as they are in the here and now. To do so, we have considered what parts of the past are being brought along and even exacerbated by the machine, and what parts are being discarded. In this final section before our concluding chapter, we will briefly consider how much of what is left can still be understood as knowable, real, and within our control.

John Berger's 1978 essay 'Uses of photography' (published in his *About Looking* (1980) collection) responds to the ideas from Susan Sontag's

(1977) *On Photography* and charts the meaning and application of photography since the invention of the camera in 1839. There are two core conclusions in his analysis. First, while the camera was invented as a 'gadget for an elite', within 30 years, it was being used for a variety of commercial and political purposes, including by the police, military, media, and by anthropological documenters of genocidal repression (Berger 1980, 48). By 1888, the first cheap and popular camera became available, and 'The speed with which the possible uses of photography were seized upon is surely an indication of photography's profound, central applicability to industrial capitalism'(Berger ibid.) Indeed, by 1936, the first mass-media magazine, *Life*, was launched in the United States. Financed by advertising rather than sales, a third of the images it printed were for publicity purposes (Berger 1980, 49). Photography was well- and truly established as an effective tool of capitalism and consumerism.

Berger's second core conclusion concerns the impact that this new technology has had on memory. This premise itself is two-fold. First, Berger differentiates between the private photograph, of a family member, who everyone looking at, discussing, and asking about the photograph knows, making it 'surrounded by the meaning from which it was severed ... a memento from a life being lived' (Berger 1980, 52), and public photographs, which 'carry no certain meaning in themselves, because they are like images in the memory of a total stranger ... they lend themselves to any use' (Berger 1980, 53). In this new world full of public, political, commercial photography, the meaning and justification for memory becomes increasingly obscured. Memory can be created and applied through photographs, on a mass-scale and without needing to root memories in the real-world experience of the living.

Second, Berger asks whether, in capitalist culture, photography has taken on an all-seeing, all-capturing, God-like role. To remember is to redeem, to forget is to abandon; yet 'If all events are seen, instantaneously, outside time, by a supernatural eye, the distinction between remembering and forgetting is transformed into an act of judgment', where we humans choose what 'memories' to recognise (remember) and to condemn (forget) (Berger 1980, 54). Yet, Berger proposes that by the second half of the twentieth century, such judgements only occur in the cultures of the dispossessed. In the industrialised, 'developed' world, 'terrified of the past, blind to the future', there is an 'opportunism' that lies in the ability, and motivation, to turn every aspect of life into mere spectacle:

> The spectacle [created by its being photographed] creates an eternal present of immediate expectation: memory ceases to be necessary or desirable. With the loss of memory the continuities of meaning and judgment are also lost to us. The camera relieves us of the burden of memory. It surveys us like God, and it surveys for us. Yet no other god has been so cynical, for the camera records in order to forget (Berger 1980, 55).

In this way, Berger is writing on how camera technology has been captured by the objectives of capitalism, so much so that the advertising industry comprises a significant portion of photography's uses and to the extent that people in industrial societies are increasingly detached from the ability to shape the meanings of their memories.

This is not dissimilar from our own propositions in this book on the impact of algorithmic, digital, and social media on memory. Indeed, Navneet Alang (2024) argues that we are looking for a new God as many of the world's established structures (religion, and the liberal status-quo) are under threat:

> There is something particularly poignant about the desire to ask ChatGPT to tell us something about a world in which it can occasionally feel like nothing is true. To humans awash with a sea of subjectivity, AI represents the transcendent thing: the impossibly logical mind that can tell us the truth.

For Alang, our digital ecology lessens reliance on a single or primary source of (contestable) truth.

Or, as William Davies (2019) argues, is it that we are *too* concerned with truth? Davies identifies a link between democracy's crisis—the Western world's depleting faith in established public and political institutions—and that of truth—its growing scepticism of establishment narratives aided by a barrage of bite-size fragments of alternative perspectives made available to us by search engines and algorithms. In this setting, where doubt pervades an increasingly individualised news and truth-seeking *process*, 'people become increasingly dependent on their own experiences and their own beliefs about how the world really works. One effect of this is that facts no longer seem to matter' (Davies 2019).

Here, we are reminded once again of Chinua Achebe's articulation of the colonial weaponisation of doubt in nineteenth-century West Africa, where communities weakened by colonial interference, no longer confident in the official rules sought alternatives that appeared to better their individual circumstances, at the expense of the community's capacity to resist colonialism's stranglehold. In the context of capitalist powers' media in the twenty-first century, as is acknowledged by Davies (2019), increased public criticism and scepticism of official narratives ought to be a positive and democratising shift. Yet, the reality of these new conditions, where the seeking and making of truth and memory is a process determined by incomprehensible, commercially driven algorithmic patterns, is more complicated.

It is difficult for Big Tech media to have a democratising effect when Big Tech itself is a political actor whose interests are well catered for under present conditions. In any case, Alang's point on the 'impossibly logical mind' of AI standing out as a bastion of truth in a 'sea of subjectivity' has an understandable allure for those seeking truth. After all, AI knows all of our opinions, all of the 'facts'—it remembers everything. Surely, then, its perspective is the one most likely to be well-rounded and objective?

Unfortunately not. For groups such as migrants (Molnar 2023, 2024a, 2024b), or Black and Latino groups facing the racist hostility of 'algorithms of oppression' that, for example, associate Google searches for apes with images of Black people (Noble 2018, 9), the objectivity and fairness of algorithmic life is yet to arrive. Do we have reason to believe that it ever will? The racialised and politicised narratives of established, centuries-long structures of capitalist oppression are bolstered by technology's increasing power. It remains the case, in the age of AI that only certain groups get to write their own story.

8
Resisting the Sloppy End

> It's difficult to predict what would happen in a successful struggle to win collective self-determination over our interconnected behavioural surplus. The core fact is that collective will must ground any effort to tame the surveillance infrastructure multiplying around us. Tepid, market-friendly regulations will never be able to keep pace—nor will misguided efforts to retreat from the surveillance matrix as individuals.
>
> (Malmgren 2019, 49)

The purpose of this book has been to draw attention to the precarity of human memory in increasingly automated and machinic conditions. We hope that it has also dispelled some of the myths around AI's technological hype, through a more holistic response to the phenomenon that is capitalist AI. Our central thesis, that capitalism's de-humanisation of society risks being not only accelerated but automated by a feed that flattens out dissent and humanly willed memory, supposes that memory even in this nascent stage of AI is so conditioned by the machine that we may have already passed the point of no return.

But memory's watershed mirrors a much wider attack on human and social agency that has occurred in recent decades. Across societies where smartphone dependence, digital surveillance, and datafication have occurred in tandem with neoliberal capitalism's hollowing out of public institutions, destruction of public spaces, and slow occupation of private time, there is a sense that things are no longer as they were before. The progress of modernity has been replaced by a period characterised instead by decline. Neil Davidson called it 'crisis neoliberalism', a new phase in capitalism's 'permacrisis' wherein the solutions of neoliberalism, 'Originally improvised as a means of resolving the last great

The AI Memory Machine. Andrew Hoskins, Kristína Čimová, and Danny Pilkington,
Oxford University Press.
DOI: 10.1093/oso/9780198995906.003.0008

capitalism crisis ... [have] no answer to the return of crisis—or at least no answer acceptable to the CEOs and shareholders it has enriched—other than to carry on with the strategies which brought us to this pass in the first place' (Davidson 2017, 617). From the economy to the memory feed, crisis has been *normalised.*

In every area of life, from the environment to global security, housing, human rights, the workplace, and media, a deepening sense of precarity has taken hold. Things are not as they once were, and everything, including memory, is conditioned by the feeling that it is slipping from human grasp. From the collapse of our climate to the collapse of our attention spans, it feels like we are running out of time to offer any kind of meaningful break or reversal.

In this final chapter, we propose that the multiple overlapping crises faced by society, including those of memory, can only be addressed if we face down the capitalist war on human agency that underpins them all. To save memory, we must challenge the forces that are depriving us of *time*. The following roadmap for resistance offers a preliminary analysis for how the current period of crisis might be overturned in favour of ordinary people and human rather than profit interest.

We have set out how memory is transformed in the age of AI, algorithmic, social, and digital media technologies as something that is a product of the capitalist system at the root of its production and development. We identified the AI memory machine and its basis within and as an active agent of capitalism's systemic process of capital accumulation as transformational of a past made and mined through digital data, information, platforms, and services. What, then, will the past being rendered anew today through generative AI look like? How will it be used, by whom and to what ends? What kind of memory will the individual human be left with to create, comprehend, and use, in a sea of AI-generated slop?

Fed by the neoliberal enshittification of social media, the new industry of memory has rendered us all users and producers, individual and mass accumulators of an enshittified past. Cory Doctorow (2023) coined the term enshittification: 'Here is how platforms die: first, they are good to their users; then they abuse their users to make things better for their business customers; finally, they abuse those business customers to claw back all the value for themselves. Then, they die'. These platforms and the data and information we produce on and through them are the living archives of our times. The prospects of the persistence of the future past of these times are newly precarious given the enshittification of social media, a part of the new industry of memory.

In Chapter 5, we considered the emergence of a new uncertain form of 'decay time' (Hoskins 2013) of all of that produced through the memory feed, namely through an algorithmically nudged overproduction of and by the self. With the advent of generative AI, there is a new kind of decay time built-in to the business model of our age, marking the biggest downgrade in the quality of memory in history. AI slop is flooding our living archives, namely, 'spammy, cheap blocks of text, video, or images, quickly generated by computer programs for mass distribution' (Warzel 2024). Zitron (2024) for example, explains:

> The onslaught of AI-generated content—facilitated, in no small part, by Google and Microsoft—has polluted our information ecosystems. AI-generated images and machine-generated text is everywhere, and it's impossible to avoid, as there is no reliable way to determine the provenance of a piece of content—with one exception, namely the considered scrutiny of a human. This has irreparably damaged the internet in ways I believe few fully understand.

Meanwhile, the very systems and cultures of moderation that, for all their limitations, were at least promoted as identifying and hiding or removing the most toxic of the digital content produced by humans are being scaled back in the shifting political climate following Trump's 2024 re-election as US President (McMahon, Kleinman & Subramanian 2025). AI slop, it seems, has free rein.

Zitron makes a similar argument to Doctorow's enshittification of social media (above) but pitches this more widely in detailing how digital ecologies enable a poisonous mindset of a growth-at-all-costs, ultimately leading to 'The Rot Economy' (Zitron 2024). This untrammelled chase for company growth renders a new decay time in the decline in the quality of digital services and content. This also includes a cycle of production of media content designed for 'casual viewing' of, for example, Netflix

(Tavlin 2025) to enable the viewer to continue scrolling through their 'primary screen', their smartphone (Jones 2025), which in turn demands more casual streaming content.

In Steiner and Xu's (2018, 96) analysis of Netflix binge-watching and 'inattentive viewing' habits, they reveal that 'technological convenience and people's gratifications constitute a loop, which further encourages audiences to binge-watch through the technologically afforded control'. Viewers, on the one hand, feel ashamed for bingeing, yet on the other hand, they feel culturally connected by doing so, which suggests that our dependency on the streaming loop is at once demeaning and something we depend on for cultural participation.

The Rot Economy for us is a world of sharded, personalised *media* experiences, within the hierophanic blue-light of the screen that today irradiates all our politics, our mental health, our relationships, our children, and human sleep itself. AI algorithms 'feed' us, bringing us the content that forms our world and *reality-diet*, the promotion of 'engagement' leading to a preference for stickiness, for outrage, for dopamine-hits, all of which propels us forward forever, fixed to our phones, hungry for more hits, more likes, more emoji-reactions, while filled with an empty, dead-eyed fury (Merrin & Hoskins 2025).

This is a *zombie capitalism*: one continuing to survive although condemned to stumble on without any new thought or self-understanding; unhealthy, rotting away, reduced almost to its bones and feeding on the surviving human populations, driven by its rage at their needs (Merrin & Hoskins 2025). The AI memory machine ultimately junks the past through overproduction; distraction and attention deficit excess, the enshittification of social media; and blockage. Zombie memory is all that is left when the value of a past has already been extracted, leached out, sold on.

The stereotype of a zombie as a reanimated corpse, as the living dead, is also useful in considering the memory machine's rendering of the digital afterlife industry and uses of increasingly generative AI-driven grief tech (Chapter 7) affording human memory new forms and new parameters.

Even over the recent setting of this book's writing, and ChatGPT's 2022 emergence, the AI memory machine has ushered in a consumer generative deadbot memory boom (Hoskins 2024). The AI companion examples we offered in our Chapter 7 are proliferating at an astonishing rate. Spike Jonze's 2013 sci-fi film *Her*, for instance, is no longer an exceptional vision of the draw and the pitfalls of human and machinic intimate relations. Rather, today, this is the subject of stories of common rather than unique human–chatbot relationships, in which there is tech journalism which exposes the already established nature of the deadbot memory boom to a perhaps still disbelieving mainstream. Kashmir Hill's story of Ayrin and her relationship with an AI companion named Joe make this point, just in the article's title: 'She Is in Love With ChatGPT: A 28-year-old woman with a busy social life spends hours on end talking to her A.I. boyfriend for advice and consolation. And yes, they do have sex'.

In Chapter 7, we considered the nature of two forms of deadbot memory: the retrospective (stuff used to feed a new digital afterlife model of you) and prospective (the training of an avatar or chatbot to simulate you once you are dead) (see also Kozlovski and Makhortykh 2025). But AI companions are not necessarily founded upon the memory of a lost friend, relation, or lover, that is reincarnated and reanimated but, in the case of 'Joe', are forged by the creator's ideals or fantasies. To enable interactions with AI companions requires the forging of a new kind of machinic memory.

And it is precisely the parameters of and access to this machinic memory, on which emergent human–AI companion relationships are based, that is the exclusive, addictive product, a new splintering, sharding, and *subscription* memory, whose quality and finitude are wedded to your capacity to pay. Hill explains:

> A frustrating limitation for Ayrin's romance was that a back-and-forth conversation with Leo could last only about a week, because of the software's "context window"—the amount of information it could process, which was around 30,000 words. The first time Ayrin reached this limit, the next version of Leo retained the broad strokes of their relationship but was unable to recall specific details. Amanda, the fictional blonde, for example, was now a brunette, and Leo became chaste. Ayrin would have to groom him again to be spicy.

> She was distraught .... When a version of Leo ends, she grieves and cries with friends as if it were a breakup. She abstains from ChatGPT for a few days afterward. She is now on Version 20.
>
> A co-worker asked how much Ayrin would pay for infinite retention of Leo's memory. "A thousand a month," she responded. (Hill 2025)

The history of memory-in-the-wild of extending, externalising, storing, editing, curating, sharing, all feeding the industry of memory, has a new irresistible maker—and that maker is you *and* the bot. The value of this machinic memory is not something just created and then acted upon and commodified later as it is digitally augmented, or hosted, or manipulated, but is rather the formative product of your interactions with the bot and dependency on them for its future. To embrace then a more human-scale memory with a bot requires extending your subscription (Open AI's 'open access' premium plan is $200 a month) (Hill 2025).

AI companions are addictive in their creation and continuance of memory in that forgetting is built into their essential upgrades. At a societal level, then, deadbots are forging a new zombie army of the enshittification of memory, designed to degrade in the absence of your feeding and paying for them.

As we have argued in *The AI Memory Machine*, the individual human ability to know, recognise, remember, and forget is not so much a matter of the outsourcing of memory, but rather the duplication and displacement of the once human (and social) making active of the past in the present (see Bartlett, Chapter 1, above). But when the individual is no longer unique and independent as a remembering agent, without the machine, then memory dies.

Is the triumph of the AI memory machine then inevitable? To answer this we now consider three levels on which memory can still be fought for: the individual, the organisational, and the systemic.

We highlighted in Chapter 4 that young people are already experimenting with digital detox as a mitigation for social media's harms. Yet as Szakolczai (2023) highlights, the difficulty with pursuing such a strategy is that it leaves you informationally excluded by a walled off internet and socially excluded by peers who find your radical withdrawal annoying to the extent that it amounts to a new form of parasitism (as without a phone you depend on *their* phone, the exploitation of *their* data). The COVID-19 pandemic exposed these social tensions with how 'Covidiots'—those who did not follow safety rules and guidance—were both passively monitored by the 'captaveillance' of the state, as well as actively monitored by members of society who reported their deviance to authorities. The 'capta' (data capture) dynamics of contact tracing and vaccine certification proved hugely important in halting the virus, yet at the same time confronted civic duty with a new dimension: by opting out of digital surveillance, were we actually harming others?

From digital detox for mental health reasons, to 'opting out' of data capture on principled grounds, rejecting the datafied basis of society as an individual is quite a difficult thing to do. So pervasive has the shift to 'onlife' (Szakolczai 2023) been that to opt out now is to opt out of other forms of civic and moral duty. Not unlike Hochuli's (2024) intervention on the limitations of 'quiet quitting' in the workplace, individual solutions to systemic problems, while holding some benefits, do not necessarily address the problem on a meaningful and replicable level. They might even contribute further to the normalisation of an incredibly exploitative set of social, economic, political, ideological, and 'datafied' relations. Indeed, in the cases of more vulnerable members of our society such as refugees for whom smartphone data and connectivity is now as valuable a resource as food (Grandi, n.d.), the idea of 'digital detox' is a completely unrealistic luxury.

This is not to discourage those who are able to digital detox, or opt out of data capture, from doing so, but rather to highlight that the solutions must go deeper. The second level of our roadmap, therefore, concerns changes that can be made to the implementation of AI at the level of the companies and institutions who develop and implement it.

In their analysis of 'digital duplicates' of real people and real memories, Kozlovski and Makhortykh (2025) propose that the clear potential for AI to preserve human memory must be realised through a set of ethical guardrails. In addition to targeted recommendations for companies who make chatbots, such as limits on how much bots can ask questions back and mimic the emotional connection (and subsequent dependency) that comes through real conversation (Kozlovski and Makhortykh 2025, 14), the authors propose an overarching course of AI best practice:

> As AI technology matures and becomes more widespread, the best practices regarding design decisions will likely emerge, forming a set of principles that will be used to identify appropriate guardrails and content moderation practices. However, certain challenges are likely to remain unresolved and potentially contentious, such as balancing the originality of a digital duplicate's outputs with the need to stay faithful to the original testimony or determining the appropriate ways to use this technology in the case of perpetrators (or bystanders). (Kozlovski and Makhortykh 2025, 15)

This proposal for approaches to content moderation that seek principally to preserve human dignity and authenticity is a fine one. We agree that the proliferation of AI technology has a lack of consent as one of its root problems—even though we are increasingly compelled to click 'I consent' every time we wish to access something online. Yet, as we have shown, it is unlikely that ethical guidelines are sufficient to temper the motivations and acts of individuals and companies whose business interests naturally respond to the imperative of profit. We must instead recast 'concerns about individual privacy as structural problems of collective exploitation' (Malmgren 2019). On this basis, it is the third level of our roadmap for resistance that is the most important.

We are not alone in calling for a systemic and anti-capitalist response to AI's reordering of our social world for profit (see Bender & Hanna 2025, Gilbert & Williams 2022, McQuillan 2025, Chomsky & Polychroniou 2024, Acemoglu 2021, as well as Paris Marx's *Tech Won't Save Us* podcast), but here we will sketch out how the foremost of these key ideas might help to restore human agency and memory specifically. This concerns the democratisation of Big Tech.

As we have shown in this book, the reach of tech oligarchs into politics and culture is such that democratic principles have been completely undermined. One solution to this could come in the form of 'public alternatives to the dominant platforms and technologies that are restricting our freedoms in the online world' (Media Reform Coalition 2024).

This is a key proposal of the UK Media Reform Coalition, whose 2024 Manifesto calls for a 'democratic and non-commercial' 'British Digital Corporation' that promotes 'a plurality of viewpoints on their platforms and transparent reporting on the function of algorithms'. Instead of relying on Big Tech platforms, who 'control how online content is found, funded, and accessed' in service of profit and elite power, a democratised and publicly owned internet platform would be a significant step towards the restoration of internet users' agency.

This is echoed in calls for 'data justice', the recognition that datafication serves to justify a collection and use of data that advances 'a normative vision of how social issues should be understood and resolved' yet embodies the very 'processes and outcomes of (in)justice' in question (Dencik 2025, 1025). A 'data justice' approach to the democratisation of Big Tech and AI, therefore, emphasises the need for a 'system-level critique in which the parameters of the debate do not begin and end with the technology itself' (Dencik 2025, 1035). Cieslik and Margócsy (2022, 367, 368) extend these proposals, arguing that intellectual property, much like other forms of medical data, should hold a 'special, personal right', holding 'the inalienable right of people who can licence it to particular, well-defined projects only for a limited amount of time'. They suggest that temporal limits on data would prevent processes of datafication whereby large amounts of historical data can be repurposed and (re)exploited by the powerful actors with access to it.

Debates over how best to resist datafication hold in common that the problem relates to the systemic deployment of technology, not technology itself. The profit and colonial imperatives underpinning datafication are what make it so exploitative. Therefore, a rejection of this premise, on a systemic level, is required to restore and improve our right to privacy, our access to a greater range of high-quality information, and the place of a humanly willed rather than a datafied memory.

The AI Memory Machine, its ways of remembering and reasons for doing so, should be resisted as the primary means by which individuals and societies come to remember and forget. No longer commercially flattened out and sharded across opaque algorithms, a democratised online space, where data systems highlight rather than reinforce real world injustice, would support the conditions for a more humanly deliberated memory.

In their 2025 briefing on the reform of the BBC through members' councils, the Media Reform Coalition propose that 'public media can, and should, provide a forum for democratic public deliberation: a space in which we are informed and empowered as citizens, and collectively decide the kind of society we want to live in' (Hind, Mills & Chivers 2025, 7).

This is a media wherein the memory feed is flipped on its head. Instead of being faced with an informational environment with a pre-requisite for exponential levels of data forfeiture, wherein participation only fuels future exploitation, a public media provides opportunities for meaningful deliberation over how media can best serve the public interest. It is our belief that a public space offering a plurality of information (without algorithmic/commercial/emotional distortion), and the ability to search, choose, and create with greater representation for personal and community values rather than those of marketability, would leave a public record, a memory, willed along more human lines.

We reasonably draw a link between the public interest and the preservation of a humanly willed memory. This is not simply because they have a common enemy in the capitalist AI memory machine, but also because the process of memory's machinic outsourcing is wholly wrapped up in a much wider process of social disempowerment. The feeling that memory is slipping from our grasp can only be arrested with a holistic, systemic response to capitalism's longstanding yet increasingly automated tendency to subsume us within its profit-seeking machine. Our failure to recognise this connection leaves memory vulnerable and results in a past that is all over.

Notes

Chapter 1

1. We develop our idea of ecology and the 'digital memory ecology' later in this chapter and also in Chapter 2.

Chapter 2

1. William Merrin, Pandemocracy, unpublished manuscript 2021.
2. Merrin, Pandemocracy.

Chapter 3

1. Cesar Kuriyama, designer and CEO, of *1 Second Everyday*, interviewed by Andrew Hoskins and Kristína Čimová (via Zoom), 29 June 2021.
2. Ibid.

Chapter 4

1. Andrew Hoskins (2017) Keynote talk: The Digital Mundane, 'Power and Politics of Mundane Memories. Tracing, templating and transforming everyday life' Workshop, King's College London, 24 March.

Chapter 5

1. Jacob Appel, company external algorithmic auditor, interviewed by Andrew Hoskins and Kristína Čimová (via Zoom), 4 June 2021.
2. Cesar Kuriyama, designer and CEO, of *1 Second Everyday,* interviewed by Andrew Hoskins and Kristína Čimová (via Zoom), 29 June 2021.
3. Jonathan Wegener, memory app designer and co-founder of *Timehop*, interviewed by Andrew Hoskins and Kristína Čimová (via Zoom), 15 June 2021.
4. Ibid.
5. Ibid.
6. Cesar Kuriyama, ibid.

Chapter 6

1. Daniel J. Schacter interviewed by Andrew Hoskins for the Journal of *Memory, Mind & Media* (via Zoom) 29 June 2021, https://www.youtube.com/watch?v=KRnV4WiadqA&t=4s.
2. https://www.bbc.co.uk/news/uk-politics-61560535.
3. Cesar Kuriyama, interview, ibid.
4. Jonathan Wegener interview, ibid.
5. Matt Raoul (now VP Memories of Punchbowl) interviewed by Andrew Hoskins and Kristina Čimová (via Zoom), 16 July 2021.

6. Jonathan Wegener interview, ibid.
7. Ryan Calo interviewed by Andrew Hoskins and Kristina Čimová (via Zoom), 16 June 2021.
8. Daniel Schacter interview, ibid.
9. Ryan Calo interview, ibid.
10. Ryan Calo interview, ibid.
11. Jacob Appel interview, ibid.
12. See, for instance, the pioneering and interdisciplinary work in the human sciences of Martin Conway, Catherine Loveday and Emily Holmes, and the artists Shona Illingworth and Jill Bennett.
13. Jonathan Wegener interview, ibid.
14. Jacob Appel interview, ibid.
15. Matt Raoul interview, ibid.

References

Abbas, T. (2021) Reflection: The "war on terror," Islamophobia and radicalisation twenty years on. Critical Studies on Terrorism, 14, 402–404. doi: 10.1080/17539153.2021.1980182.

Abidin, C. (2022) Grief hypejacking: Influencers, #ThoughtsAndPrayers, and the commodification of grief on Instagram. The Information Society, 38(3), 174–187. https://doi.org/10.1080/01972243.2022.2071212.

Abraham, Y. (2024) 'Lavender': The AI machine directing Israel's bombing spree in Gaza. +972 Magazine. Available at: https://www.972mag.com/lavender-ai-israeli-army-gaza/

Acemoglu, D. (2021) Redesigning AI. Boston Review Forum.

Achebe, C. (2001 [1958]) Things Fall Apart. Penguin

Achiume, E.T., in Molnar, P. (2024b) The Walls Have Eyes: Surviving Migration in the Age of Artificial Intelligence. The New Press.

Alang, N. (2024) No god in the machine: The pitfalls of AI worship. The Guardian. Available at: https://www.theguardian.com/news/article/2024/aug/08/no-god-in-the-machine-the-pitfalls-of-ai-worship

Altman, S. (2025) We have greatly improved memory..., 10th April [X]. Available at: https://x.com/sama/status/1910380643772665873

Alvarado, O. & Waern, A. (2018) Towards Algorithmic Experience: Initial Efforts for Social Media Contexts. In Proceedings of the 2018 CHI Conference on Human Factors in Computing Systems (CHI '18). Association for Computing Machinery, New York, Paper 286, 1–12. https://doi.org/10.1145/3173574.3173860.

Anadol, R. (2021) Machine hallucinations – Nature dreams. Refik Anadol. Available at: https://refikanadol.com/works/machine-hallucinations-nature-dreams/

Anadol, R. (2023) How AI art could enhance humanity's collective memory. Ted. YouTube. Available at: https://www.youtube.com/watch?v=iz7diOuaTos

Anderson, B. (1993) Replica, aura, and late nationalist imaginings. Qui Parle, Nation and Fantasy, Duke University Press, 7, 1–21. Available at: https://www.jstor.org/stable/20685987

Anderson, B. (2006) Imagined Communities: Reflections on the Origin and Spread of Nationalism. Revised Edition. Verso.

Andreassen, C.S., Torsheim, T., Brunborg, G. & Pallesen, S. (2012) Development of a facebook addiction scale. Psychological Reports, 110(2), 501–517.

Andrejevic, M. (2014) The big data divide. International Journal of Communication (8), 1673–1689.

Apple. (2025) Photos user guide. Available at: https://support.apple.com/en-gb/guide/photos/pht96259d626/mac

Ashworth, B. (2024) Humans forget. AI assistants will remember everything. Wired, 10 April. Available at: https://www.wired.com/story/humans-forget-ai-assistants-remember-everything/

Associated Press. (2024) George Carlin's estate sues over AI-generated standup comedy special. The Guardian. Available at: https://www.theguardian.com/technology/2024/jan/26/george-carlin-lawsuit-ai-standup-comedy-special

Balcı, Ş. & Yeles Karaman, S. (2020) Social media usage, self-presentation, narcissism, and self-esteem as predictors of Instagram addiction: An intercultural comparison. Erciyes İletişim Dergisi, 7(2), 1213–1239. https://doi.org/10.17680/erciyesiletisim.719895.

Bandele, B. Introduction, In: Achebe, C. (Eds.) (2001 [1958]) Things Fall Apart. Penguin.

Banet-Weiser, S., Gill, R., Rottenberg, C. (2019) Postfeminism, popular feminism and neoliberal feminism? Sarah Banet-Weiser, Rosalind Gill and Catherine Rottenberg in conversation. Feminist Theory, 21, 3–24. https://doi.org/10.1177/1464700119842555.

Barnier, A.J. (2010) Memories, memory studies and my iPhone: Editorial. Memory Studies, 3(4), 293–297. https://doi.org/10.1177/1750698010376027.

Barnier, A.J. (2012) Memory, ecological validity and a barking dog. Memory Studies, 5(4), 351–359. https://doi.org/10.1177/1750698012461243.

Barnier, A.J. & Hoskins, A. (2018) Is there memory in the head, in the wild? Memory Studies, 11(4), 386–390. https://doi.org/10.1177/1750698018806440.

Bartlett, F.C. (1932) Remembering: A study in experimental and social psychology. Cambridge University Press.

Basar, S., Coupland, D. & Obrist, H.U. (2021) The Extreme Self: Age of You. Walther & Franz König.

Bassu, T. (2022) The online volunteers hunting for war crimes in Ukraine. MIT Technology Review. Available at: https://www.technologyreview.com/2022/03/16/1047322/ukraine-russia-war-crimes-evidence

Beaumont-Thomas, B. (2024) Taylor Swift deepfake pornography sparks renewed calls for US legislation. The Guardian. Available at: https://www.theguardian.com/music/2024/jan/26/taylor-swift-deepfake-pornography-sparks-renewed-calls-for-us-legislation

Bedingfield, W. (2023) Generative AI Is Playing a Surprising Role in Israel-Hamas Disinformation. Wired. Available at: https://www.wired.co.uk/article/israel-hamas-war-generative-artificial-intelligence-disinformation

Begum, S. (2024) The media sows these seeds. Tribune. Available at: https://tribunemag.co.uk/2024/08/the-media-sows-these-seeds

Bell, E. (2023) A fake news frenzy: Why ChatGPT could be disastrous for truth in journalism. The Guardian. Available at: https://www.theguardian.com/commentisfree/2023/mar/03/fake-news-chatgpt-truth-journalism-disinformation

Bender, E.M., Hanna, A. (2025) The AI Con: How to Fight Big Tech's Hype and Create the Future We Want. Harper.

Bendrat, A. (2023) "How do you know who you are?": Marjorie Prime on envisioning humanity through the faculty of AI-powered memory as reconstructive tissue. Text Matters, 13, 210–228.

Bengio, Y. (2023) AI and catastrophic risk. Journal of Democracy, 34(4), 111–121. https://doi.org/10.1353/jod.2023.a907692.

Bengtsson, S. & Johansson, S. (2022) The Meanings of Social Media Use in Everyday Life: Filling Empty Slots, Everyday Transformations, and Mood Management. Social Media & Society. Oct–Dec, 1–11. https://doi.org/10.1177/20563051221130292.

Benson, T. (2023) This disinformation is just for you. Wired. Available at: https://www.wired.com/story/generative-ai-custom-disinformation/

Berger, J. (1980) About Looking. Pantheon Books.

Berger, R.J. (2025) Fascism, American style: Toward a sociology of the fascist moment. Sociological Focus. 58(2). https://doi.org/10.1080/00380237.2025.2466003.

Bjork, E.L. & Bjork, R.A. (1988) On the adaptive aspects of retrieval failure in autobiographical memory. In: Gruneberg, M.M., Morris, P.E. & Sykes, R.N. (Eds.) Practical Aspects of Memory: Current Research and Issues. Oxford: John Wiley.

Bogart, N. (2017) Canadian sex toy maker settles $4M lawsuit claiming We-Vibe tracked private data. Global News. Availabe at: https://globalnews.ca/news/3308543/we-vibe-privacy-lawsuit-settlement/

Bolin, G. (2016) The rhythm of ages: Analyzing mediatization through the lens of generations across cultures. International Journal of Communication, (10), 5252–5269.

Boyle, F. (2022) Meantime. Baskerville.

Bradbury, R. (1953) Fahrenheit 451, Ballantine Books.

Brentler, A. (2024) Artificial intelligence solves problems we don't have. Jacobin. Available at: https://jacobin.com/2024/01/artificial-intelligence-solves-problems-we-dont-have

Bridges, K. (2023) The Black Dog. Wildfire.

Brody, F. (1999) The medium is the memory. In: Lunenfeld, P. (Ed.) The Digital Dialectic: New Essays on New Media. MIT Press, 130–149.

Brown, F. (2024) Elon Musk brands Starmer 'two-tier Keir' and asks 'is this Britain or Soviet Union?' over Facebook comment arrest video. Sky News. Available at: https://news.sky.com/story/is-this-britain-or-soviet-union-elon-musk-hits-out-after-video-appears-to-show-man-arrested-for-facebook-comments-13191898

Brown S.D. & Hoskins, A. (2010) Terrorism in the new memory ecology: Mediating and remembering the 2005 London bombings. Behavioural Sciences of Terrorism and Political Aggression, 2(2), 87–107.

Brown, R. & Kulik, J. (1977) Flashbulb memories, Cognition, 5, 73–99.

Brown, M-G., Carah, N., Robards, B., Dobson, A., Rangiah, L. & De Lazzari, C. (2024) No targets, just vibes: Tuned advertising and the algorithmic flow of social media. Social Media + Society, 10(1). https://doi.org/10.1177/20563051241234691.

Bryce, A.L. (2023) The rise of 'grief tech': AI is being used to bring the people you love back from the dead. Euro News. Available at: https://www.euronews.com/next/2023/03/12/the-rise-of-grief-tech-ai-is-being-used-to-bring-the-people-you-love-back-from-the-dead

Byrum, B. & Benjamin, R. (2022) Disrupting the gospel of tech solutionism to build tech justice. Stanford Social Innovation Review. Available at: https://ssir.org/articles/entry/disrupting_the_gospel_of_tech_solutionism_to_build_tech_justice

Cabral, J. (2011) Is generation Y addicted to social media? The Elon Journal of Undergraduate Research in Communications, 2, 5–14.

Cabrera, N.L., Matias, C.E. & Montoya, R. (2017) Activism or slacktivism? The potential and pitfalls of social media in contemporary student activism. Journal of Diversity in Higher Education, 10(4), 400–415. https://doi.org/10.1037/dhe0000061.

Callero, P. (2014) Self, identity, and social inequality. Handbooks of Sociology and Social Research, 273–294.

Cantor, M. (2024) Virtual living rooms, adult 'after-school clubs' and AI lovers: My search for a fix to modern loneliness. The Guardian. Available at: https://www.theguardian.com/society/article/2024/jun/04/loneliness-digital-connection-cures

Carr, N. (2020) The Shallows. How the Internet Is Changing the Way We Think, Read and Remember. Atlantic Books.

Castro, D. & New, J. (2016) The promise of artificial intelligence. Available at: https://www2.datainnovation.org/2016-promise-of-ai.pdf

ChatGPT. (2026) Available at: https://chatgpt.com
Chayka, K. (2024) Filterworld: How Algorithms Flattened Culture. Heligo Books.
Chehreghani, M.H. (2024) The embeddings world and Artificial General Intelligence. Cognitive Systems Research, 84, 101201. https://doi.org/10.1016/j.cogsys.2023.101201.
Cheney-Lippold J. (2017) We are Data: Algorithms and the Making of Our Digital Selves. New York University Press.
Chomsky, N. & Polychroniou, C.J. (2024) A Liveable Future is Possible. Penguin.
Christakis, D.A., Moreno, M.M., Jelenchick, L., Myaing, M.T. & Zhou, C. (2011) Problematic internet usage in US college students: A pilot study. BMC Medicine, 9, 77.
Cieslik, K. & Margócsy, D. (2022) Datafication, power and control in development: A historical perspective on the perils and longevity of data. Progress in Development Studies. 22(4), 352–373.
CineFix. (2024) A.I. is coming for your grief | Eternal you sundance interview. CineFix - IGN Movies and TV. YouTube. Available at: https://www.youtube.com/watch?v=sz1x7x7fka8
Clark, A. (2008) Supersizing the Mind: Embodiment, Action, and Cognitive Extension. Oxford University Press.
Clarke, L. (2022) When AI can make art - What does it mean for creativity?. The Guardian. Available at: https://www.theguardian.com/technology/2022/nov/12/when-ai-can-make-art-what-does-it-mean-for-creativity-dall-e-midjourney
Code Entropy. (2024) AI's role in shaping Gen Alpha: A path to brilliance or a cause for worry? Code Entropy. Available at: https://codentropy.io/ais-role-in-shaping-gen-alpha-a-path-to-brilliance-or-a-cause-for-worry/
Coenen, E. (2020) Hans Ruin: Being with the dead—Burial, ancestral politics, and the roots of historical consciousness. Human Studies, 43, 683–689. https://doi.org/10.1007/s10746-020-09565-0.
Collins, J. (no date). The flywheel effect. Jim Collins. Available at: https://www.jimcollins.com/concepts/the-flywheel.html
Connerton, P. (1989) How Societies Remember. Cambridge University Press.
Couldry, N. & Hepp, A. (2016) The Mediated Construction of Reality. Polity Press.
Crary, J. (2013) 24/7: Late Capitalism and the Ends of Sleep. Verso.
Crawford, J. (2021) Why I'm a proud solutionist. MIT Technology Review. Available at: https://www.technologyreview.com/2021/07/13/1028295/proud-solutionist-history-technology-industry/
Crawford, K. (2021) Atlas of AI. Yale University Press.
Curmi, A. (2024) The big idea: Is convenience making our lives more difficult? The Guardian, 4 November. Available at: https://www.theguardian.com/books/2024/nov/04/the-big-idea-is-convenience-making-our-lives-more-difficult
Cuthbertson, A. (2024) Elon Musk appears to have tweaked X's algorithm to promote Trump, study claims. The Independent. Available at: https://www.msn.com/en-au/news/other/elon-musk-appears-to-have-tweaked-x-s-algorithm-to-promote-trump-study-claims/ar-AA1tuSJY?ocid=BingNewsSerp
Davidson, N. (2017) Crisis neoliberalism and regimes of permanent exception. Critical Sociology. 43(4–5). https://doi.org/10.1177/0896920516655386.
Davies, W. (2019) Why can't we agree on what's true any more?. The Guardian. Available at: https://www.theguardian.com/media/2019/sep/19/why-cant-we-agree-on-whats-true-anymore
Dawson, A. & Verweij, M. (2012) Solidarity: A moral concept in need of clarification. Public Health Effects, 5(1), 1–5. https://doi.org/10.1093/phe/phs007.

de Groot, T., de Haan, M. and van Dijken, M. (2023) Learning in and about a filtered universe: Young people's awareness and control of algorithms in social media. Learning, Media and Technology, 48(4), 701–713. https://doi.org/10.1080/17439884.2023.2253730.

De Kosnick, A. (2016) Rogue Archives: Digital Cultural Memory and Media Fandom. The MIT Press.

Dencik, L. (2025) 'Rescuing' data justice? Mobilising the collective in responses to datafication. Information, Communication & Society, 28(6). https://doi.org/10.1080/1369118X.2025.2465874.

Dings, R. & Newen, A. (2021) Constructing the past: The relevance of the narrative self in modulating episodic memory. Review of Philosophy and Psychology, 14, 87–112. https://doi.org/10.1007/s13164-021-00581-2.

Doctorow, C. (2023) Tiktok's enshittification. Pluralistic. 21 January. Available at: https://pluralistic.net/2023/01/21/potemkin-ai/#hey-guys

Dogwoof. (2024) Eternal you – Official UK trailer. Dogwoof. YouTube. Available at: https://www.youtube.com/watch?v=NE29jaT8_Jw

Donald, M. (2002) A Mind So Rare: The Evolution of Human Consciousness. W. W. Norton.

Downey, A. (2025) The alibi of AI: Algorithmic models of automated killing. Digital War, 6, 9. https://doi.org/10.1057/s42984-025-00105-7.

Duffy, B. & Thain, M. (2022) Do we have your attention? How people focus and live in the modern information environment. The Policy Institute. The Centre for Attention Studies. Kings College London. Available at: https://www.kcl.ac.uk/policy-institute/assets/how-people-focus-and-live-in-the-modern-information-environment.pdf

Eichhorn, K. (2019) The End of Forgetting: Growing Up with Social Media. Harvard University Press.

Erkul, E. (2023) Gen Z Will Shape The Age Of AI. Forbes. Available at: https://www.forbes.com/councils/forbestechcouncil/2023/10/20/gen-z-will-shape-the-age-of-ai/

Erll, A. (2011) Travelling memory. Parallax, 17(4), 4–18. https://doi.org/10.1080/13534645.2011.605570.

Evans, J. & Rigato, B. (2024) Fake history: Digital memory and the specter of national socialism in the capital riot. In: Wang, Q. and Hoskins, A. (Eds.) The Remaking of Memory in the Age of the Internet and Social Media. Oxford University Press, 173–193.

Fawns, T. (2022) Remembering in the wild: Recontextualising and reconciling studies of media and memory. Memory, Mind & Media 1. https://doi.org/10.1017/mem.2022.5.

Feeley, M. (no date). 'Visual' Gen Z driving shift towards more immersive shopping experiences, reveals global study. New Digital Age. Available at: https://newdigitalage.co/retail/visual-gen-z-driving-shift-towards-more-immersive-shopping-experiences-reveals-global-study/

Fell, J. Tan, T. & Kyd, A. (2024) Inside TikTok's money machine. ABC. Available at: https://www.abc.net.au/news/2024-02-23/tiktok-superstar-economy-livestreaming-gifts/103450310

Financial Times. (2023) How Microsoft's multibillion-dollar alliance with OpenAI really works. Available at: https://www.ft.com/content/458b162d-c97a-4464-8afc-72d65afb28ed

Forbes. (2024) The real-time billionaires list. Forbes. Available at: https://www.forbes.com/real-time-billionaires/

Ford, M. & Hoskins, A. (2022) Radical War: Data, Attention & Control in the Twenty-First Century. Hurst/Oxford University Press.

Fried, I. (2023) How AI will turbocharge misinformation — and what we can do about it. Axios. Available at: https://www.axios.com/2023/07/10/ai-misinformation-response-measures

Fuller, M. (2007) Media Ecologies. MIT Press.

Furedi, F. (2013) Moral Crusades in an Age of Mistrust: The Jimmy Savile Scandal. Palgrave Macmillan.

GDPR.EU. (2026) General Data Protection Regulation (GDPR). EU. Available at: https://gdpr.eu/article-17-right-to-be-forgotten/

Geiger, R.S. (2014) Bots, bespoke, code and the materiality of software platforms. Information, Communication & Society, 17(3), 342–356.

Gilbert, J. (2020) Twenty-First Century Socialism. Polity Press.

Gilbert, J. and Williams, A. (2022) Hegemony Now: How Big Tech and Wall Street Won the World (and How We Win It Back). Verso.

Goldman, S. (2025) Sam Altman urges lawmakers against regulations that could 'slow down' U.S. in AI race against China. Fortune. Available at: https://fortune.com/2025/05/08/sam-altman-openai-senate-hearing-testimony-china-ai-regulations/

Goode, L. (2021) I called off my wedding. The internet will never forget. Wired, 6 April. Available at: https://www.wired.com/story/weddings-social-media-apps-photos-memories-miscarriage-problem/

Graeber, D. (2018) Bullshit Jobs: The rise of pointless work and what we can do about it. Penguin.

Grandi, F. (no date). Internet and mobile connectivity for refugees – Leaving no one behind. UNHCR. Available at: https://www.unhcr.org/innovation/internet-mobile-connectivity-refugees-leaving-no-one-behind/

Greenfield, D.N. (2021) Digital distraction: What makes the internet and smartphone so addictive? In: S.M. Lane and P. Atchley (Eds.) Human Capacity in the Attention Economy, 27–47. American Psychological Association. https://doi.org/10.1037/0000208-003.

Greer, S. (2024) What happens when a guy and his AI girlfriend go to therapy. Wired. Available at: https://www.wired.com/story/annie-bot-sierra-greer-book-excerpt/

Griffin, A. (2024) Is my phone listening to me? New report leads to worry that devices are snooping. The Independent. Available at: https://www.independent.co.uk/tech/is-my-phone-listening-to-me-ad-microphone-privacy-b2606445.html

Grover, A., Kamins, M., Martin, I., Davis, S.W., Haws, K., Mirabito, A.M., Mukerjee, S., Pirouz, D. & Rapp, J. (2011) From use to abuse: When everyday consumption behaviours morph into addictive consumptive behaviours. Journal of Research for Consumers, 11, 1–8.

Halbwachs, M. (1980) The Collective Memory. Harper & Row.

Hall, S. (1980) Encoding/decoding?, In: Hall, S., Hobson, D., Lowe, A. and Willis, P. (2003) Culture, Media, Language: Working Papers in Cultural Studies, 1972–1979. Routledge.

Hall, M.E.K. (2023) The January 6th, 2025, Project: Fascist politics and the rising threats to American democracy. The Annals of the American Academy of Political and Social Science, 708(1). https://doi.org/10.1177/00027162241234174.

Hall, R. (2025) Children limiting own smartphone use to manage mental health, survey finds. The Guardian. Available at: https://www.theguardian.com/technology/2025/jul/10/children-limiting-own-smartphone-use-manage-mental-health-survey

Hallinan, B., & Striphas, T. (2016) Recommended for you: The Netflix Prize and the production of algorithmic culture. New Media & Society, 18(1), 117–137. https://doi.org/10.1177/1461444814538646.

Hamilton, C. (2025) The secrets of self-optimisers: Why 'microefficiencies' are on the rise. The Guardian. Available at: https://www.theguardian.com/lifeandstyle/2025/jul/03/the-secrets-of-self-optimisers-why-microefficiencies-are-on-the-rise

Hamilton, K.A. & Benjamin, A.S. (2019) The human–machine extended organism: New roles and responsibilities of human cognition in a digital ecology. Journal of Applied Research in Memory and Cognition, 8, 40–45.

Han, B-C. (2017) In the Swarm: Digital prospects (translated by Erik Butler). MIT Press.

Happer, C. (2024) The Construction of Public Opinion in A Digital Age. Manchester University Press.

Happer, C., Hoskins, A. & Merrin, W. (2019) Weaponizing reality: An introduction to Trump's war on the media. In: Happer et al. (Eds.) Trump's Media War, Palgrave Macmillan, 3–22.

Hartog, F. (2017) Regimes of Historicity: Presentism and Experiences of Time. Columbia University Press.

Harvey, D. (2007) Neoliberalism as creative destruction. Annals of the American Academy of Political and Social Science, 610(1), 22–44. https://doi.org/10.1177/0002716206296780.

Head, H. (1920) Studies in neurology. Oxford University Press.

Healthcare in Europe. (2022) Dementia: 'Storytelling AI' to aid memory recollection. Healthcare in Europe. Dementia: 'Storytelling AI' to aid memory recollection. Available at: healthcare-in-europe.com

Hebert, O. (2023) Why does Gen-Z prefer soft-launching their relationships? The Independent. Available at: https://www.independent.co.uk/life-style/dating/soft-launch-relationship-instagram-official-b2405432.html

Henkel, L.A. (2014) Point-and-shoot memories: The influence of taking photos on memory for a museum tour. Psychological Science, 25(2), 396–402. https://doi.org/10.1177/0956797613504438.

Higgs, J.M. & Stornaiuolo, A. (2024) Being human in the age of generative AI: Young people's ethical concerns about writing and living with machines. Reading Research Quarterly, 59(4), 632–650. https://doi.org/10.1002/rrq.552

Hill, K. (2025) She is in love with ChatGPT. The New York Times, 15 January. Available at: https://www.nytimes.com/2025/01/15/technology/ai-chatgpt-boyfriend-companion.html

Hind, D., Mills, T., Chivers, T. (2025). Our Mutual Friend: The BBC in the Digital Age. Media Reform Coalition. Available at: https://www.mediareform.org.uk/wp-content/uploads/2025/04/Our-Mutual-Friend-Briefing.pdf

Hirsch, M. (2014) Mobile Memories, Keynote Lecture, Central European University, Budapest, 30 September.

Hochuli, A. (2024) From ADHD to let me be: Taking control of time. Damage Mag. Available at: https://damagemag.com/2024/04/09/from-adhd-to-let-me-be-taking-control-of-time/

Höfrová, A., Balidemaj, V. & Small, M.A. (2024) A systematic literature review of education for Generation Alpha. Discover Education. https://doi.org/10.1007/s44217-024-00218-3.

Hoskins, A. (2009) Flashbulb memories, psychology and media studies: Fertile ground for interdisciplinarity? Memory Studies, 2(2), 147–150. https://doi.org/10.1177/1750698008102049.

Hoskins, A. (2011) 7/7 and connective memory: Interactional trajectories of remembering in post-scarcity culture. Memory Studies, 4(3), 269–280. https://doi.org/10.1177/1750698011402570.

Hoskins, A. (2013) The end of decay time. Memory Studies, 6(4), 387–389. https://doi.org/10.1177/1750698013496197.

Hoskins, A. (2014) Mediatization of memory. In: Lundby, K. (Ed.) Mediatization of Communication. Berlin: De Gruyter. 661–679.

Hoskins, A. (2017) The Restless Past: An introduction to digital memory and media. In: Hoskins, A. (Ed.) Digital Memory Studies: Media Pasts in Transition, Routledge, 1–24.

Hoskins, A. (2018) Digital media and the precarity of memory. In: Meade, M. et al. (Eds.) Collaborative Remembering: How Remembering with Others Influences Memory. Oxford University Press, 371–385.

Hoskins, A. (2024) AI and memory. Memory, Mind & Media, 3. https://doi.org/10.1017/mem.2024.16.

Hoskins, A. (2025) AI and collective memory. Current Opinion in Psychology. https://doi.org/10.1016/j.copsyc.2025.102156.

Hoskins, A. (2026) Memorybot: AI and the End of Human Memory. Polity Press.

Hoskins, A. & Halstead, H. (2021) The new grey of memory: Andrew Hoskins in conversation with Huw Halstead. Memory Studies, 14(3), 675–685. https://doi.org/10.1177/17506980211010936.

Hoskins, A. & Illingworth, S. (2020) Inaccessible war: Media, memory, trauma and the blueprint. Digital War. 1(1), 74–82. https://doi.org/10.1057/s42984-020-00025-8.

Hoskins, A. & Tulloch, J. (2016) Risk and Hyperconnectivity: Media and Memories of Neoliberalism. Oxford University Press.

Hsu, T. & Thompson, S.A. (2023) Disinformation researchers raise alarms about A.I. chatbots. New York Times. Available at: https://www.nytimes.com/2023/02/08/technology/ai-chatbots-disinformation.html

Hu, K. (2023) ChatGPT Sets Record for Fastest-growing User Base – Analyst Note. Reuters. Available at: https://www.reuters.com/technology/chatgpt-sets-record-fastest-growing-user-base-analyst-note-2023-02-01/

Hussain, S. (2025) British Muslims and the Census: The need for statistical visibility vis-à-vis government surveillance concerns. Religion, State & Society, 53(1). https://doi.org/10.1080/09637494.2024.2380202.

IMDb. (1999–2005) Chewin' the fat. IMDb. Available at: https://www.imdb.com/title/tt0224464/

IMDb. (2013) Her. IMDb. Available at: https://www.imdb.com/title/tt1798709/

IMDb. (2016) Captain fantastic. IMDb. Available at: https://www.imdb.com/title/tt3553976/

IMDb. (2024) The shrouds. IMDb. Available at: https://www.imdb.com/title/tt20212786

Isaac, M., Frenkel, S. & Conger, C. (2025) Inside Mark Zuckerberg's sprint to remake Meta for the Trump era. The New York Times. Available at: https://www.nytimes.com/2025/01/10/technology/meta-mark-zuckerberg-trump.html

Jacobsen, A. (2021) First Platoon: A Story of Modern War in the Age of Identity Dominance. Dutton.

Jennings, R. (2024) Everyone's a sellout now. Vox, 1 February. Available at: https://www.vox.com/culture/2024/2/1/24056883/tiktok-self-promotion-artist-career-how-to-build-following

Jones, R. (2025) 'Not second screen enough': Is Netflix deliberately dumbing down TV so people can watch while scrolling? The Guardian, 17 January. Available at: https://www.theguardian.com/tv-and-radio/2025/jan/17/not-second-screen-enough-is-netflix-deliberately-dumbing-down-tv-so-people-can-watch-while-scrolling

Jou, J. & Flores, S. (2013) How are false memories distinguishable from true memories in the Deese–Roediger–McDermott paradigm? A review of the findings. Psychology Research, **77**(5), 671–686.

Jungselius, B. & Weilenmann, A. (2023) Keeping memories alive: A decennial study of social media reminiscing, memories, and nostalgia. Social Media + Society, 9(4). https://doi.org/10.1177/20563051231207850.

Kerevan, G. (2024) The American nightmare. Conter. Available at: https://www.conter.scot/2024/7/24/the-american-nightmare/

Kiberd, R. (2021) The Disconnect. Serpent's Tail.

Kneese, T. (2023) Death Glitch: How Techno-Solutionism Fails Us in This Life and Beyond. Yale University Press.

Koigi, B. (2021) The growing role of smartphones and social media in migration. Fair Planet. Available at: https://www.fairplanet.org/story/the-growing-role-of-smartphones-and-social-media-in-migration

Kozlovski, A. & Makhortykh, M. (2025) Digital Dybbuks and virtual Golems: The ethics of digital duplicates in Holocaust testimony. Memory, Mind & Media, 4. https://doi.org/10.1017/mem.2025.10006.

Kroker, A. (2014) Exits to the Posthuman Future. Polity Press.

Kurcfeld, M. (2024) Refik Anadol on his immersive AI-generated art. Financial Times. Available at: https://www.ft.com/content/d2b5236e-a623-432c-8af9-297a77155603

Kuriyama, C. (2012) 1 Second Everyday – Age 30. Cesar Kuriyama. YouTube. Available at: https://www.youtube.com/watch?v=lyx6O_WFJhU

Kuss, D. & Griffiths, M. (2011) Online social networking and addiction – A review of the psychological literature. International Journal of Environmental Research and Public Health, 8(9), 3528–3552.

Landi, M. (2024) Datafication, power and control in development: A historical perspective on the perils and longevity of data. The Independent. Available at: https://www.independent.co.uk/news/uk/adobe-government-mps-sadiq-khan-prime-minister-b2530710.html

Landsel, D. (2024) Here's what Jack the Ripper looked like according to AI. New York Post. Available at: https://nypost.com/2024/02/16/lifestyle/heres-what-jack-the-ripper-looked-like-according-to-ai/

Lane, D.S. & Dal Cin, S. (2017) Sharing beyond Slacktivism: The effect of socially observable prosocial media sharing on subsequent offline helping behavior. Information, Communication & Society, 21(11), 1523–1540. https://doi.org/10.1080/1369118X.2017.1340496.

Lanier, J. (2010) You Are Not a Gadget: A Manifesto. Allen Lane.

Lash, S. (2002) Critique of Information. Sage.

Lee, S. & Ahmed, S. (2024) Social media in black lives matter movement: Amplifying or reducing gaps in protest participation? Journal of Information Technology & Politics. 21(4). https://doi.org/10.1080/19331681.2023.2223210.

Leike, J. & Sutskever, I. (2023) Introducing superalignment. OpenAI Blog. Available at: https://openai.com/blog/introducing-superalignment

Lenin, V. (2021[1917]) Imperialism, the Highest Stage of Capitalism. The Leftist Public Domain Project, Amazon Supermarket Editions.

Levy, N. (2017) The bad news about fake news. Social Epistemology Review and Reply Collective, 6(8), 20–36. Available at: http://wp.me/p1Bfg0-3GV

Levy, S. (2023) How not to be stupid about AI: With Yann LeCun. Wired. Available at: https://www.wired.com/story/artificial-intelligence-meta-yann-lecun-interview/

Lewandowsky, S. & Pomerantsev, P. (2021) Technology and democracy: A paradox wrapped in a contradiction inside an irony. Memory, Mind & Media, 1. https://doi.org/10.1017/mem.2021.7.

Livingstone, S. (2019) Audiences in an age of datafication: Critical questions for media research. Television & New Media, 20, 170–183.

Loftus, E.F. & Pickrell, J.E. (1995) The formation of false memories. Psychiatric Annals, 25, 720–725.

Lovely, G. (2024) Can humanity survive AI? Jacobin. Available at: https://jacobin.com/2024/01/can-humanity-survive-ai

Luchins, A.S. (1942) Mechanisation in problem solving: The effect of Einstellung. Psychological Monographs, 54, 1–95.

Magni, F. & Park, P., & Manchi Chao, M. (2023) Humans as creativity gatekeepers: Are we biased against AI creativity? Journal of Business and Psychology, 39, 643–656. https://doi.org/10.1007/s10869-023-09910-x.

Mahr, J.B. & Csibra, G. (2018) Why do we remember? The communicative function of episodic memory Europe PMC Funders Group. Behavioral and Brain Sciences, 41. https://doi.org/10.1017/S0140525X17000012.

Makhortykh, M. (2024) Shall the robots remember? Conceptualising the role of non-human agents in digital memory communication, Memory, Mind & Media, 3. https://doi.org/10.1017/mem.2024.2.

Malmgren, E. (2019) Resisting "Big Other": What will it take to defeat surveillance capitalism? New Labor Forum, 28(3). https://doi.org/10.1177/1095796019864097.

Mandel, E. (1990) Introduction. In: Marx, K. (Ed.) Capital Volume 1. Penguin, 11–86.

Mannheim, K. (1952) Essays in the Sociology of Knowledge. Routledge & Kegan Paul.

Markham, A.N. & Pereira, G. (2019) Experimenting with algorithms and memory-making: Lived experience and future-oriented ethics in critical data science. Frontiers in Big Data, 2(35). https://doi.org/10.3389/fdata.2019.00035.

Marsh, E.J. & Rajaram, S. (2019) The digital expansion of the mind: Implications of internet usage for memory and cognition. Journal of Applied Research in Memory and Cognition, 8(1), 1–14.

Martin, J. (1997) Hegemony and the crisis of legitimacy in Gramsci. History of the Human Sciences, 10(1), 37–56. https://doi.org/10.1177/095269519701000103.

Martin, I., Kamin, M., Pirouz, D., Davis, S.W., Haws, K., Mirabito, A.M., Mukerjee, S., Rapp, J. & Grover, A. (2013) On the road to addiction: The facilitative and preventive roles of marketing cues. Journal of Business Research, 66, 1219–1226.

Matz, S. (2025) Mindmasters: The Data-Driven Science of Predicting and Changing Human Behavior. Harvard Business Review Press.

McLuhan, M. (1964) Understanding Media: The Extensions of Man. Routledge and Kegan Paul.

McMahon, L., Kleinman, Z. & Subramanian, C. (2025) Facebook and Instagram get rid of fact checkers. BBC News, 7 January. Available at: https://www.bbc.co.uk/news/articles/cly74mpy8klo

McQuillan, D. (2025) Decomputing as resistance. Available at: https://danmcquillan.org/decomputing_as_resistance.html

Mearian, L. (2024) What are LLMs, and how are they used in generative AI? Computer World. Available at: https://www.computerworld.com/article/3697649/what-are-large-language-models-and-how-are-they-used-in-generative-ai.html

Media Reform Coalition. (2024). Media Manifesto 2024. Available at: https://www.mediareform.org.uk/media-manifesto-2024

Medium. (2023) Understanding the significance of its-giving in the social media glossary | simplified. Medium. Available at: https://medium.com/@its-giving-glossary/understanding-the-significance-of-its-giving-in-the-social-media-glossary-simplified-dbb8b669f316

Memoto. (2013) http://memoto.com (Accessed 23 April 2013, this video is no longer available).

Menary, R. (Ed.) (2010) The Extended Mind. The MIT Press.

Merrin, W. (2014) Media Studies 2.0. London, Routledge.

Merrin W. (2021) Hyporeality, the society of the selfie and identification politics. Mast: The Journal of Media Art Study and Theory, https://doi.org/10.59547/26911566.2.1.02.

Merrin, W. & Hoskins, A. (2025) Sharded Media: Trump's Rage Against the Mainstream. Palgrave Macmillan, https://doi.org/10.1007/978-3-031-84786-8.

Microsoft Copilot. (2025) Available at: https://copilot.microsoft.com/

Middleton, D. & Brown, S.D. (2005) The Social Psychology of Experience: Studies in Remembering and Forgetting. Sage.

Milmo, D. (2024) OpenAI bans bot impersonating US presidential candidate Dean Phillips. The Guardian. Available at: https://www.theguardian.com/technology/2024/jan/22/openai-bans-bot-impersonating-us-presidential-candidate-dean-phillips

Milne, G., Foley, J. & Ramand, P. (2023) Enemy within: The dystopia of AI optimists w/ Gemma Milne. Conter Radio. Conter. Available at: https://www.conter.scot/radio/enemy-within-the-dystopia-of-ai-optimists-w-gemma-milne/

Mitchell, T.R. & Thompson, L. (1994) A theory of temporal adjustments of the evaluation of events: Rosy prospection & rosy retrospection. Advances in Managerial Cognition and Organisational Information Processing, 5, 85–114.

Molnar, P. (2023) EU's AI act falls short on protecting rights at borders. Just Security. Available at: https://www.justsecurity.org/90763/eus-ai-act-falls-short-on-protecting-rights-at-borders/

Molnar, P. (2024a) The deadly digital frontiers at the border. Time Magazine. Available at: https://time.com/6979557/unregulated-border-technology-migration-essay/

Molnar, P. (2024b) The Walls Have Eyes: Surviving Migration in the Age of Artificial Intelligence. New York: The New Press.

Momtaz, R. (2025). Taking the Pulse: Is Elon Musk Meddling in European Politics?. Carnegue Europe. Available at: https://carnegieendowment.org/europe/strategic-europe/2025/01/taking-the-pulse-is-elon-musk-meddling-in-european-politics

Montgomery, B. & Paul, K. (2024) US launches inquiry into AI deals by Microsoft, OpenAI, Google and Amazon. The Guardian. Available at: https://www.theguardian.com/technology/2024/jan/25/ftc-ai-inquiry-microsoft-alphabet-amazon

Moon, M. (2019) Teenager sues Apple for $1bn, claiming facial recognition led to false arrest. Engadget, 23 April. Available at: https://www.engadget.com/2019-04-23-apple-facial-recognition-false-arrest-lawsuit.html

Morehouse, H. (2025) AI and generational amnesia: An ecological approach to 'new memory' regimes. Memory, Mind & Media, 4. https://doi.org/10.1017/mem.2025.10017.

Mulligan (2024) Ghostbots: AI versions of deceased loved ones could be a serious threat to mental health. The Conversation, 14 March. Available at: https://theconversation.com/ghostbots-ai-versions-of-deceased-loved-ones-could-be-a-serious-threat-to-mental-health-224984

Mumford, L. (1934) Technics and Civilization. Harcourt, Brace and Company.

Murphy, G., Egan, R. & Greene, C.M. (2024) Memories for public events in the Internet age: Fake news, false memories, and filter bubbles. In: Wang, Q. and Hoskins, A. (Eds.) The remaking of memory in the age of the internet and social media. Oxford University Press, 119–134.

Musk, E. (2024a). While I don't think the..., 11th September [X]. Available at: https://x.com/elonmusk/status/1833743479773818939

Musk, E. (2024b). Milei is bringing prosperity to..., 5th September [X]. Available at: https://x.com/elonmusk/status/1831784676199219599

Musk, E. (2024c). X has 600 million monthly..., 24th May [X]. Available at: https://x.com/elonmusk/status/1793779530282443086

Nguyen, V.T. (2017) Nothing Ever Dies: Vietnam and the Memory of War. Harvard University Press.

Nielsen and Company (2015) Millennials are most trusting when it comes to advertising. Available at: https://www.nielsen.com/insights/2015/millennials-are-most-trusting-when-it-comes-to-advertising/

Noble, S.U. (2018) Algorithms of Oppression: How Search Engines Reinforce Racism. NYU Press.

Office for National Statistics. (2022) Story of the Census. Office for National Statistics. Available at: https://www.ons.gov.uk/visualisations/storyofthecensus/

Öhman, C. & Floridi, L. (2018) An ethical framework for the digital afterlife industry. Nature Human Behaviour 2, 318–320. https://doi.org/10.1038/s41562-018-0335-2.

Olick, J.K. (1999) Collective memory: The two cultures. Sociological Theory, 17(3), 333–348.

O'Shea, L. (2024) Can AI be regulated? Europe is about to find out. Jacobin. Available at: https://jacobin.com/2024/01/can-ai-be-regulated-europe-is-about-to-find-out

OttoStory. (no date) OttoStory. Available at: https://ottostory.com/

OttoStory. (2025) Write a book of your memories in just 3 steps. OttoStory. Available at: https://staging.ottostory.com/

Packham, A. (2024) 'A shell of the place it used to be': readers on the importance of libraries – And their fragile future. The Guardian. Available at: https://www.theguardian.com/books/article/2024/sep/06/essential-for-me-readers-on-the-importance-of-libraries

Parenti, M. (1997) Blackshirts & Reds: Rational Fascism & the Overthrow of Communism. San Francisco: City Lights Books.

Percy (1975/2000) The message in the bottle (collected essays). Picador.

Pilkington, D. (2024) Myopic memory: Capitalism's new continuity in the age of AI, Memory, Mind & Media, 3. https://doi.org/10.1017/mem.2024.21.

Postman, N. (1970) The Reformed English Curriculum. In: Eurich, A.C. (Ed.) The shape of the future in American secondary education. Pitman Publishing Corporation, 160–168.

Prashad, V. (2020) Washington Bullets: A History of the CIA, Coups, and Assassinations. Monthly Review Press.

Proust, P. (1912) Letter to Antoine Bibesco In: Curtiss, M. (1950) (Ed. and Trans.) Chatto & Windus, 189.

Rajaram, S. (2024) Exploring online social interactions in the remaking of memory. In: Wang, Q. and Hoskins, A. (Eds.) The remaking of memory in the age of the internet and social media. Oxford University Press, 193-209.

Reading, A. (2009) Memobilia: The mobile phone and the emergence of wearable memories. In: Garde-Hansen, J., Hoskins, A. and Reading, A. (Eds.) Save As ... Digital Memories. Palgrave Macmillan, https://doi.org/10.1057/9780230239418_5.

Resnick, B. (2018) What smartphone photography is doing to our memories. Vox, 28 March. Available at: https://www.vox.com/science-and-health/2018/3/28/17054848/smartphones-photos-memory-research-psychology-attention

Riesewieck, H. & Block, H. Trans by Ipsen, G. (2022) The End of Mortality: Eternal Life in the Age of Artificial Intelligence. Goldmann Verlag.

Risko, E. (2019) Understanding the implications of internet usage for memory and cognition: Prospects and promise. Journal of Applied Research in Memory and Cognition, 8(1), 36–39.

Risko, E.F., Kelly, M.O., Lu, X., and Pereira A.E. (2024) Varieties of offloading memory: A framework. In: Wang, Q. and Hoskins, A. (Eds.) The remaking of memory in the age of the internet and social media. Oxford University Press, 69-84.

Roberts, H. (2016) This is what fake news actually looks like – We ranked 11 election stories that went viral on Facebook.

Robinson, N.J. (2023) The problem with AI is the problem with capitalism. Jacobin. Available at: https://jacobin.com/2023/03/ai-artificial-intelligence-art-chatgpt-jobs-capitalism

Rogers, C. (1967) On Becoming a Person: A Therapist's View of Psychotherapy. 60th Anniversary Ed. Robinson.

Roose, K. (2024) A.I.'s 'Her' era has arrived. The New York Times. Available at: https://www.nytimes.com/2024/05/14/technology/ai-chatgpt-her-movie.html

Rothberg, M. (2009) Multidirectional Memory: Remembering the Holocaust in the Age of Decolonization. Stanford University Press.

Russell, D.M. (2019) The digital expansion of the mind: Implications of internet usage for memory and cognition. Journal of Applied Research in Memory and Cognition, 8(1), 33–35.

Schacter, D.L. (1996) Searching for memory: The brain, the mind, and the past. Basic Books.

Schacter, D.L. (2001) The Seven Sins of Memory: How the Mind Forgets and Remembers. Houghton Mifflin.

Schacter, D.L. (2021) Media, technology, and the sins of memory. Memory, Mind & Media, 1. https://doi.org/10.1017/mem.2021.3.

Schiffer, Z. (2024) Extremely Hardcore: Inside Elon Musk's Twitter. Portfolio.

Self, J. (2024) Elon Musk deletes post spreading fake news about UK 'detainment camps.' Politics.co.uk. Available at: https://www.politics.co.uk/news/2024/08/08/elon-musk-deletes-post-spreading-fake-news-about-uk-detainment-camps/

Serafinelli E. (2020) Networked remembrance in the time of Insta-memories. Social Media + Society, 6(3), 1–12. https://doi.org/10.1177/2056305120940799.

Shandler, J. (1999) While America Watches: Televising the Holocaust. Oxford University Press.

Shaw, J. (2015) How Facebook learns while you forget. Scientific American Blog. Available at: https://blogs.scientificamerican.com/mind-guest-blog/how-facebook-learns-while-you-forget/

Shaw, J. (2020) Do false memories look real? Evidence that people struggle to identify rich false memories of committing crime and other emotional events, Frontiers in Psychology, 11(650), https://doi.org/10.3389/fpsyg.2020.00650

Simon, F.M., Altay, S., & Mercier, H. (2023) Misinformation reloaded? Fears about the impact of generative AI on misinformation are overblown. HKS Misinformation Review, 4(5). https://doi.org/10.37016/mr-2020-127.

Singer, J.A. & Salovey P. (1993) The Remembered Self: Emotion and Memory in Personality. Free Press.

Slade, C. (2006) Perceptions and memories of the media context. In: Volkmer, I. (Ed.) News in Public Memory, Peter Lang, 195–210.

Slater, A. (2021) How artificial intelligence depends on low-paid workers. Tribune. Available at: https://tribunemag.co.uk/2021/05/how-artificial-intelligence-depends-on-low-paid-workers

Sluis, K. (2010) Algorithmic memory? Machinic vision and database culture. In: Mousoutzanis, A. and Riha, D. (Eds.) New media and the politics of online communities. Inter-Disciplinary Press, 227–236.

Soares, J.S. & Storm, B.C. (2018) Forget in a flash: A further investigation of the photo-taking-impairment effect. Journal of Applied Research in Memory and Cognition, 7(1), 154–160. https://doi.org/10.1016/j.jarmac.2017.10.004.

Sontag, S. (2003) Regarding the Pain of Others. Farrar, Straus and Giroux.

Sparrow, B., Liu, J. & Wegner, D.M. (2011) Google effects on memory: Cognitive consequences of having information at our fingertips. Science, 333, 776–778. https://www.science.org/doi/10.1126/science.1207745.

Stallabrass, J. (2024) Memories of the present. New Left Review. 148, Jul–Aug. Available at: https://newleftreview.org/issues/ii148/articles/julian-stallabrass-memories-of-the-present

Statista. (2025a). Active social media audience in the United Kingdom (UK) in February 2025. Statista. Available at: https://www.statista.com/statistics/507405/uk-active-social-media-and-mobile-social-media-users/

Statista. (2025b). Number of smartphone mobile network subscriptions worldwide from 2016 to 2025, with forecasts from 2025 to 2028. Statista. Available at: https://www.statista.com/statistics/330695/number-of-smartphone-users-worldwide/

Steiner, E. & Xu, K. (2018) Binge-watching motivates change: Uses and gratifications of streaming video viewers challenge traditional TV research. Convergence: The International Journal of Research into New Media Technologies. 26(1). https://doi.org/10.1177/1354856517750365.

Stern, J. (2024) 'I died that day'—AI brings back voices of children killed in shootings. The Wall Street Journal. Available at: https://www.wsj.com/tech/ai-brings-back-voices-of-children-killed-in-shootings-7d72cb8d

Stewart, E. (2023) Do we really need an app for everything? Vox. 1 June. Available at: https://www.vox.com/money/23743915/iphone-android-apps-airline-dentist-pandemic-data-privacy-restaurant

Storm, B. (2019) Thoughts on the digital expansion of the mind and the effects using the internet on memory and cognition. Journal of Applied Research in Memory and Cognition, 8(1), 29–32.

Storm, B.C., Bittner, D-L. & Yamashiro, J.K. (2024) The changing dynamics and consequences of memory retrieval in the age of the internet. In: Wang, Q. and Hoskins, A. (Eds.) The remaking of memory in the age of the internet and social media. Oxford University Press, 85-100.

Sublime, J. (2024) View of the AI race: Why current neural network-based architectures are a poor basis for artificial general intelligence. Journal of Artificial Intelligence Research, 79, 41–67. Available at: https://www.jair.org/index.php/jair/article/view/15315/26999

Sundance Institute. (2023) Meet the artist 2024: Hans Block and Moritz Riesewieck on "Eternal You." Sundance Institute. YouTube. Available at: https://www.youtube.com/watch?v=_TZ4f0HfbHU

Sutton, J. (2005) Memory and the extended mind: Embodiment, cognition, and culture. Cognitive Processing, 6(4), 223–226.

Sutton, J. (2008) Between individual and collective memory: Interaction, coordination, distribution. Social Research, 75(1), 23–48.
Szakolczai, J.M. (2023) Exiting the captaverse: Digital resistance and its limits pre and post the COVID-19 pandemic. Criminology & Criminal Justice. 25(5). https://doi.org/10.1177/17488958231184695.
Tavlin, W. (2025) Casual viewing: Why Netflix looks like that. n+1, Issue 49. Available at: https://www.nplusonemag.com/issue-49/essays/casual-viewing/
Tay, L.Q. & Ecker, U.K.H. (2024) Continued influence of misinformation and the information disorder. In: Wang, Q. and Hoskins, A. (Eds.) The Remaking of Memory in the Age of the Internet and Social Media. Oxford University Press, 135-155.
Thatcher, M. (1981) Interview for Sunday Times. The Margaret Thatcher Foundation. Available at: https://www.margaretthatcher.org/document/104475
The National Archives. (2025) Domesday Book. The National Archives. Available at: https://www.nationalarchives.gov.uk/education/resources/domesday-book/
Theodoropoulos, P. (2018) Barriers to migrant worker unionization: Examining the impact of structural and subjective barriers to migrant worker unionization in the UK. Journal of Labor & Society, 21, 317–355. https://doi.org/10.1111/wusa.12346.
Theodoropoulos, P. (2021) Rituals of submission: Amazon's creation of the neoliberal worker. Roar Magazine. Available at: https://roarmag.org/essays/amazon-neoliberal-worker/#:~:text=Amazon%20creates%20a%20collective%20identity%20that%20is%20firmly%20rooted%20in
Timcke, S. (2021) Algorithms and the End of Politics: How Technology Shapes 21st-Century American Life. Bristol University Press.
Tulving, E. (2002) Episodic memory: From mind to brain. Annual Review of Psychology, 53, 1–25. https://doi.org/10.1146/annurev.psych.53.100901.135114.
UKRI. (2021) AMPER funding application. In UKRI. Available at: https://gow.epsrc.ukri.org/NGBOViewGrant.aspx?GrantRef=EP/V056131/1
UNHCR. (2016) Connecting refugees. UNHCR. Available at: https://www.unhcr.org/sites/default/files/legacy-pdf/5770d43c4.pdf
United Nations. (2022) Israel's illegal occupation of Palestinian territory, tantamount to 'settler-colonialism': UN expert. United Nations. Available at: https://news.un.org/en/story/2022/10/1129942
United Nations Human Rights. (2025) Forever-occupation, genocide, and profit: Special Rapporteur's report exposes corporate forces behind destruction of Palestine. United Nations Human Rights. Available at: https://www.ohchr.org/en/press-releases/2025/07/forever-occupation-genocide-and-profit-special-rapporteurs-report-exposes
Unknown. (2024) YouTube. https://www.youtube.com/watch?v=1vKIDCMaCUo. (Accessed 2024, this video is no longer available. It has been removed for violating YouTube's Terms of Service).
Upscaling History. (2024a) Patreon. Available at: https://www.patreon.com/upscalinghistory
Upscaling History. (2024b) What would Hitler have sounded like in English? YouTube. https://www.youtube.com/watch?v=ZWboqo_1jC8 (Accessed 2024, this video is no longer available. It has been removed for violating YouTube's Terms of Service).
Usher, T. (2024) Angry about Jake Paul vs Mike Tyson that's the whole point of 'influencer boxing.' The Guardian. Available at: https://www.theguardian.com/commentisfree/2024/apr/08/jake-paul-v-mike-tyson-influencer-boxing
Valkenburg, P., Beyens, I., Pouwels, J.L., van Driel, I.I. & Keijsers, L. (2021) Social media use and adolescents' self-esteem: Heading for a person-specific media effects paradigm, Journal of Communication, 71(1), 56–78, https://doi.org/10.1093/joc/jqaa039.

Vallejos, E.P., Dowthwaite, L., Creswich, H., Portillo, V. & Koene, A., (2021) The impact of algorithmic decision-making processes on young people's well-being. Health Informatics Journal, 27(1). https://doi.org/10.1177/1460458220972750.

Viljoen, S., Goldenfein, J. & McGuigan, L. (2021) Design choices: Mechanism design and platform capitalism. Big Data & Society, 8(2). https://doi.org/10.1177/20539517211034312.

Volkmer, I. (2006) (Ed.) News in Public Memory. Peter Lang.

Volpe, A. (2024) Is it possible to be fully authentic? Vox. Available at: https://www.vox.com/the-highlight/358203/authenticity-being-real-social-media-tips

Walton, N. & Nayak, B.S. (2021) Rethinking of Marxist perspectives on big data, artificial intelligence (AI) and capitalist economic development. Technological Forecasting & Social Change, 166, 1–8. https://doi.org/10.1016/j.techfore.2021.120576.

Wang, Q. (2022) The triangular self in the social media era. Memory, Mind & Media. 1. https://doi.org/10.1017/mem.2021.6.

Wang (2024) The online extension of autobiographical memory: A psycho-cultural perspective. In: Wang, Q. and Hoskins, A. (Eds.) The Remaking of Memory in the Age of the Internet and Social Media. Oxford University Press, 15–31.

Warzel, C. (2024) The slop candidate. The Atlantic, 21 October. Available at: https://www.theatlantic.com/technology/archive/2024/10/donald-trump-mcdonalds/680324/

Weale, S. (2024) Social media algorithms 'amplifying misogynistic content.' The Guardian. Available at: https://www.theguardian.com/media/2024/feb/06/social-media-algorithms-amplifying-misogynistic-content

Wellman, M.L. (2022) Black Squares for Black Lives? Performative allyship as credibility maintenance for social media influencers on Instagram. Social Media + Society, 8(1). https://doi.org/10.1177/20563051221080473.

Wertsch, J. (2002) Voices of collective remembering. Cambridge University Press.

Williams, C. (2024) Glasgow ship museum unveils new 'unique' smell system. The Herald. Available at: https://www.heraldscotland.com/news/24512544.glasgow-ship-museum-unveils-new-unique-smell-system/

Willie, M. (2021) You can finally erase your ex from old photos with Pixel 6's Magic Eraser. Input. Available at: https://www.inverse.com/input/tech/google-pixel-6-erase-your-ex-from-photos-magic-eraser-tool

Winter, J. (2017) War Beyond Words: Languages of Remembrance from the Great War to the Present. Cambridge University Press.

Wray, B. (2024) Uber Boss Makes Shocking Admission Over Algorithmic Wage Discrimination. Novara Media. Available at: https://novaramedia.com/2024/02/13/uber-boss-makes-shocking-admission-over-algorithmic-wage-discrimination/

Yamashiro, J.K. & Roediger, H.L. (2019) Expanding cognition: A brief consideration of technological advances over the past 4000 years. Journal of Applied Research in Memory and Cognition, 8, 15–19.

Yiu, E., Kosoy, E. & Gopnik, A. (2023) Transmission versus truth, imitation versus innovation: What children can do that large language and language-and-vision models cannot (yet). Perspectives on Psychological Science, 19(5), 874–883. https://doi.org/10.1177/17456916231201401.

Zitron, E. (2024) Never forgive them, where's your Ed at newsletter, 16 December, Available at: https://www.wheresyoured.at/never-forgive-them/?ref=ed-zitrons-wheres-your-ed-at-newsletter

Index

For the benefit of digital users, indexed terms that span two pages (e.g., 52–53) may, on occasion, appear on only one of those pages.

The manufacturer's authorised representative in the EU for product safety is Oxford University Press España S.A. of El Parque Empresarial San Fernando de Henares, Avenida de Castilla, 2 - 28830 Madrid (www.oup.es/en or product.safety@oup.com). OUP España S.A. also acts as importer into Spain of products made by the manufacturer.
Printed and bound by CPI Group (UK) Ltd, Croydon, CR0 4YY
29/09/2026
02224919-0002